WWW.MOSHIMONSTERS.COM

Published by Puffin 2013
A Penguin Company
Penguin Books Ltd, 80 Strand, London, WC2R 0RL, UK
Penguin Books Australia Ltd, 707 Collins Street, Melbourne,
Victoria 3008, Australia.
Penguin Group (NZ), 67 Apollo Drive, Rosedale, Auckland
0632, New Zealand (a division of Pearson New Zealand Ltd)

Make illustrations by Helen Hurry
Photography by Neil Hall
Food testing by Ann Reynolds

ALWAYS LEARNING   **PEARSON**

Contents

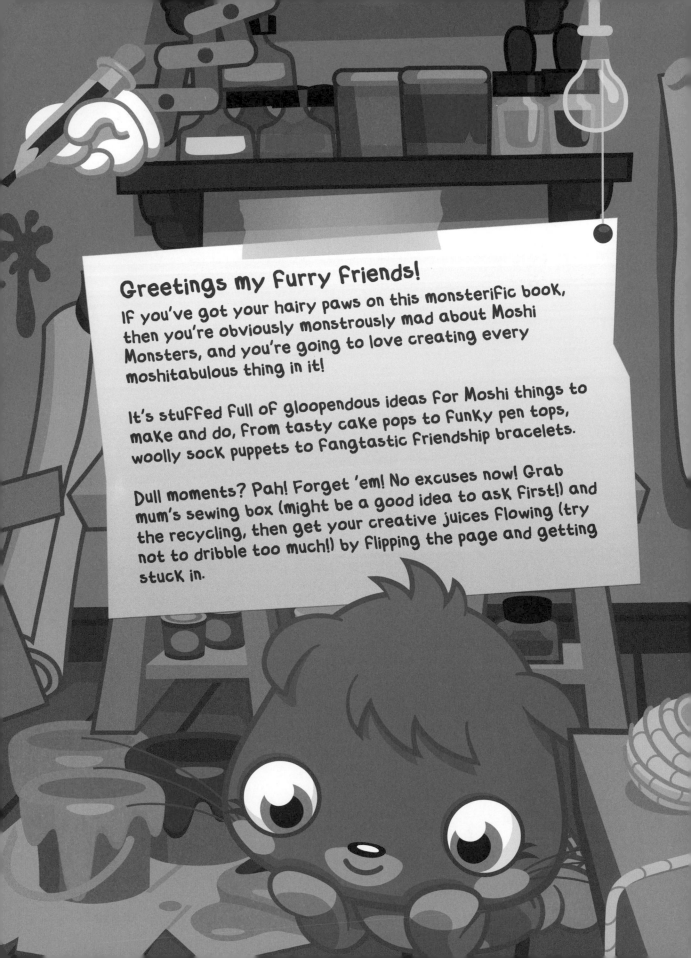

Greetings my furry friends!

If you've got your hairy paws on this monsterific book, then you're obviously monstrously mad about Moshi Monsters, and you're going to love creating every moshitabulous thing in it!

It's stuffed full of gloopendous ideas for Moshi things to make and do, from tasty cake pops to funky pen tops, woolly sock puppets to fangtastic friendship bracelets.

Dull moments? Pah! Forget 'em! No excuses now! Grab mum's sewing box (might be a good idea to ask first!) and the recycling, then get your creative juices flowing (try not to dribble too much!) by flipping the page and getting stuck in.

How to make a paper concertina

Lots of the things in this book need a concertina fold, so here's how to get it right!

1. Start with a long rectangular piece of paper. If you are making the pages for a notebook, photo album or scrapbook, you will need to stick (with sticky tape) several sheets of paper together, in a row, so that they form a very long rectangle.

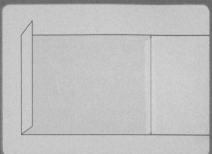

2. Hold your paper horizontally. Fold the left edge of the paper over to the right, to the width you want the strip or page to be.

3. Turn the paper over.

4. Now fold the folded section back on to itself, to the same width of the first fold.

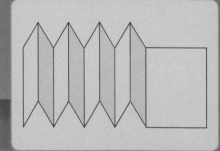

5. Turn the paper back over again and repeat steps 2 to 4 until all the paper is folded up.

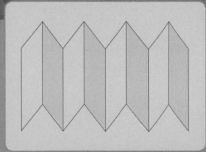

6. This is your concertina. You can now use it for the pages of a book, or to make a rosette shape or a cake case.

Scare Force One

Mwaaah haa-haa! Make your own *Scare Force One* and impress Dr. Strangeglove and the C.L.O.N.C. gang.

MOSHI TIP – How to make papier mâché

Take one part water and two parts glue, and mix together in a large bowl until you have a smooth paste. Gather as many old newspapers as you can and tear them into strips. Each strip should be about 2.5cm wide and 15cm long. Now you're ready to begin pasting the paper on to your mould!

1. Blow up an oval-shaped balloon. Cover with papier mâché. Now make your cabin base, by mixing together equal parts of PVA glue to water and torn up cardboard tube. Squish the mixture together to create a pulp.

2. Mould the pulp onto the base of the papier mâché balloon in the shape of the cabin. Leave to dry, then cover with a mixture of PVA glue and white paint. When it is completely dry, push a pin through it to pop the balloon inside.

3. Cut four wings out of navy card. Leave a tab at either end to hold each wing in place.

4. Now draw the above pattern onto the pointed end of the balloon. Paint the first pattern shape purple; the next a paler purple.

5. Paint the rest of the balloon navy blue.

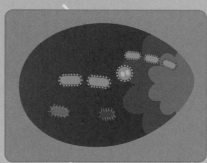

6. When dry, paint the windows, patches and goo cannons onto both sides of the balloon, as shown in the picture.

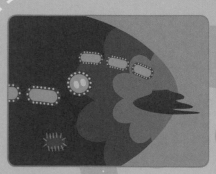

7. At the pointed end of the papier mâché balloon, make a small slit and slide a wing in. Repeat for the other three wings.

You Will Need

Balloon
Papier maché
PVA glue
Water
Cardboard tube
Paints (blues, orange,
    purple, yellow, white)
Navy and orange card
Paintbrushes
Egg boxes
Coloured pens
Scissors
Navy pipe cleaners
Yellow pompom

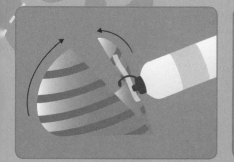

8. Make the airship's nose by cutting a semi-circle out of orange card. Draw stripes on it with a purple pen. Curl round to form a cone and stick in place.

9. Now cut out five egg cups from an egg box. Paint them turquoise and add detail. Make a small hole near the bottom in each and push in the navy pipe cleaners.

10. Take two of the egg cups and bend a pipe cleaner around the open edge of each. Glue them securely onto the cups. Stick one to the bottom of the balloon and one on top.

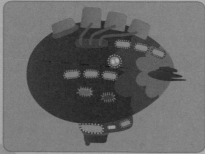

11. Now glue the other three egg cups in position (as shown above). Cut three holes in the orange shape painted on the side of the airship, and push the pipe cleaners from each egg cup into these holes.

12. Paint C.L.O.N.C. logo and cabin details onto the airship and leave to dry. Finally, glue the little yellow pompom onto the end of the stripped cone. Gloopendous!

2 Cake Pops

Sink your fangs into these bite-sized treats – once you pop, you won't stop! Monsterific!

Sponge

1. Pre-heat your oven to 190°C/Gas Mark 5. Grease and line two 20-cm/8-inch cake tins with baking parchment.

2. Cream together the butter and sugar until light and fluffy, then gradually beat in your egg mixture with a little of your measured flour until fully combined.

3. Fold in the remaining flour with a metal spoon and divide the mixture evenly between the tins, then bake in the oven for 20–25 minutes. Remove from the oven and cool on a wire rack.

Cake pops

1. Crumble both cakes into a mixing bowl. In a separate bowl beat together your butter, icing sugar and orange extract until light and fluffy.

2. Combine the cakes and icing to make a light dough. Cover with cling film and leave in the fridge for twenty minutes. Then roll the dough into medium-sized balls and place them on to a lined baking sheet.

3. Carefully melt 50g/1¾oz of your chocolate in a bowl in a microwave. Dip the lollypop stick tips into the melted chocolate, spear the cake balls, rest them on the baking sheet and return them to the fridge for 10 minutes.

4. Divide the remaining chocolate into 3 small bowls and melt in the microwave. Add a different food colouring to each bowl, depending on which character(s) you're creating.

5. Get your cake pops and carefully dip them into your melted coloured chocolate until fully coated. Leave to dry a little before using the coloured icing to create your characters' faces.

To decorate your cake pop like Scrumpy:

green food colouring for head
black icing for hat, moustache
and eyes
white icing for eyes
red icing for mouth and nose

To decorate your cake pop like Cherry Bomb:

red food colouring for head
green icing for fuse
white icing for eyes
black icing for eyebrows

To decorate your cake pop like Penny:

yellow food colouring
for head
orange icing for edging,
mouth and cheeks
black and white icing
for eyes

MOSHI TIP
Melt a little
chocolate and use
it to 'glue' your
characters'
features on.

McNulty's Secret File

Psst! Keep your secrets safe under the watchful eye of this Undercover YapYap.

You Will Need

Cardboard
A4 paper
Scissors
Sticky tape
PVA glue
Paintbrush
Newspaper
Paints
Old Fabric
Pencil
Ribbon
Pens

Fabric edging on the spine and triangular pieces of fabric on the corners make this file look clawsome!

1. Take two pieces of A4 card and lay a piece of A4 paper on to each. Tape the top, bottom and one side of each to create two pockets.

2. Glue strips of newspaper over both sides of your pieces of cardboard – but don't paste over your pocket openings! Leave to dry, then paint. Allow the paint to dry then cover with a layer of glue. These painted cardboard rectangles will be the front and back cover of your Secret File.

3. Place the two painted cover pieces side by side with the open pockets face down and facing each other. Glue a strip of fabric down the middle to make a spine.

4. Ask an adult to pierce two holes for you through each part of the cover with a pencil, about 5cm apart and 2cm from the edge. Thread a piece of ribbon through them to secure your file, then decorate the cover.

5. Shhhh! Don't tell anyone, but your Secret File is now ready to use. Fill it with all your secret monsterific Moshi stuff!

Tiki's Treasure Box

Tell that pesky Tiki to keep that pilfering beak out of this box so your trinkets don't go walkabout!

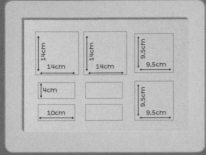

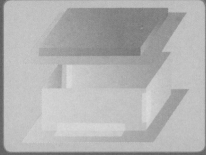

1. On the corrugated card, measure out the base and four sides of the box. Measure out three squares for the lid, one the same size as the base, the other two slightly smaller.

2. Sticky tape your box together. Glue the smaller lid squares to the underside of the main lid square. The smaller bit needs to fit within the walls of the box.

3. Cover the whole treasure box (and the lid separately) with a layer of papier mâché. Check the lid fits.

4. Let the box and lid dry in a warm, airy place.

5. Paint the box and lid with a base coat of colour (you might find it needs a second coat of paint).

6. Decorate your box then let your Moshling-tastic treasure box dry before filling it with precious things! Don't let Tiki see!

Your box needn't be square – experiment with different shapes and sizes.

You Will Need

Corrugated card
Scissors
Sticky tape
Newspaper
PVA glue
Paints
Paintbrush

Moshi TV Studio

Put on your own sizzlin' show at the Moshi TV Studios! Can you score top marks from Tyra Fangs?

1. Stand your shoebox on its side, then cut an opening at each end so your performers can get on and off their stage.

2. Choose a colour for your backdrop. Cut your coloured paper to fit and glue it into the back of your shoebox.

You Will Need

Shoebox
Scissors
Thin white card
Coloured paper
Felt-tip pens and
    crayons
PVA glue
Sticky tape
Wooden chopsticks

3. Use a piece of thin white card to create the set and the Moshi TV Studios sign – the glitzier the better! Colour in your design with the felt-tip pens and crayons, then cut it out.

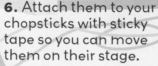

4. Glue it in place and secure any tricky bits with sticky tape if needed.

6. Attach them to your chopsticks with sticky tape so you can move them on their stage.

5. Now to make your actors! Draw their outlines on the thin white card, making sure they're not too big (or small) for your stage. Colour them in and cut them out.

SUBMIT YOUR VIDEO

moshi TV STUDIOS

Gather your furry friends together and put on a monsterific show! Tyra thinks you're FANGTASTIC!

Holga Photo Album

Say cheese, strike a pose and make your snaps Happy Snappies by sticking them in this clawsome album!

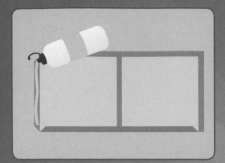

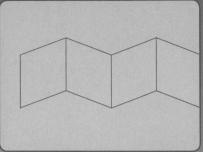

You Will Need

Scissors
Thick card
PVA glue
Brightly coloured/
    patterned paper
Two pieces of ribbon
Glitter gems
Pictures
Photographs

1. Cut two equal-sized pieces of card. Turn the paper you're using for your album cover face down. Glue on the card pieces, leaving a small gap between them, then neatly fold the paper's edges over and glue them down too.

2. Make a concertina of paper slightly smaller than your cover to form your album's pages (see the introduction for tips on how to concertina your paper).

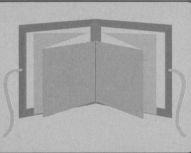

3. Glue a piece of ribbon to the inside edge of the front cover and one to the inside edge of the back cover. You can tie them together to keep your album closed.

4. Next glue in your concertina pages.

5. Add glitter gems and a picture of your choice to decorate the cover. Now it's time to stick your fangtastic photos in your snaptastic album!

Big Bad Bill

Zommer

No. 5

Rockin' Furi

Diavlo

MOSHI TIP

Why not use a concertinaed strip of funky wrapping paper for your album pages to save having to stick pieces of paper together?

Strike a pose and become an instant Monstar with Tyra's tips:

Right before the camera flashes, pretend you just saw something funny, or someone told a joke. (But don't laugh so hard you blow Toad Soda out of your nose like Roary Scrawl did once . . .)

Relax and think happy thoughts (unless you're Simon Growl . . .)

To make sure you really look your best for the camera, don't forget to take a trip to my spa on Ooh La Lane!

Eggsellent!

Surprise your mum by popping this box of Moshling eggs in the fridge! Ha, ha, ha! Splat-tastic!

You Will Need

- 6 eggs
- An eggbox
- A pin
- A bowl
- PVA glue
- Paintbrush
- Coloured tissue paper
- Paints
- Paper
- Felt-tip pens
- Coloured pipe cleaners
- Pom poms

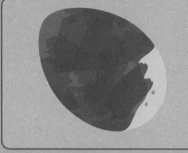

2. Paint each egg with glue and cover with coloured tissue paper of your choice, depending on which Moshlings you're creating. Allow to dry, then paint with a base colour.

3. Paint on the Moshlings' faces. If you prefer, draw them onto white paper, colour them in, then cut them out and glue on to the eggs.

1. Ask an adult to help you carefully prick a tiny hole in both ends of each of your six eggs. Holding the egg over a bowl, put the top hole gently to your mouth and blow. The egg white and yolk will slowly drip out of the bottom hole.

4. Add the finishing touches with coloured pipe cleaners, pompoms or other craft items

MOSHI TIP

Why not try covering your eggs with foil or patterned papers to make some mystery Moshling eggs?

Super Moshi Eye Mask

Attention all Super Moshis! Your mission is to make this super eye mask. Are you up to the challenge?

You Will Need

Pins
Thin card
Red felt
Scissors
Red ribbon

1. Trace the eye mask template below onto a piece of thin card. Cut it out, then carefully pin it to the red felt.

2. Cut out the felt around the template, then cut out the slits for eyes. Remove the card template and pins.

3. Cut two lengths of ribbon, long enough to tie round your head. Stick them to either side of the mask. You are now ready to don your Super Moshi disguise! Grab your cloak and get going on your next mission. Good luck, my furry friend!

Trace this template to make your Super Moshi mask.

Glump Cakes

Quick! Scoff these moshi-licious cupcakes before Dr. Strangeglove's naughty minions do!

You Will Need

150g/5½oz plain flour
60g/2oz cocoa powder
1 tbsp mild curry powder
60g/2oz butter
200ml/7fl oz water
100ml/3½fl oz buttermilk
1 egg

For the Icing:

50g/1¾oz unsalted butter, room temperature
200g/7oz icing sugar, sifted
3 tbsp coconut milk
1 drop yellow food colouring

Makes 12 cupcakes

1. Preheat your oven to 190°C/Gas Mark 5, and line a 12-hole cupcake tin with paper cases.

2. Sift your flour, cocoa and curry powder into a bowl and beat in your butter.

3. Gradually add your water and buttermilk until fully combined, then beat in your egg.

4. Pour the mixture into a measuring jug and fill each cake case to the top. The mixture will be quite watery so be careful not to spill it.

5. Put the tin in the oven and bake for fifteen to twenty minutes. These cupcakes are very moist so they will still be a little soft when you remove them.

6. When ready, remove the cakes from the oven and leave them to cool on a wire rack.

7. While they cool, make your icing by beating together the butter, sugar, coconut milk and colouring until light and fluffy.

8. When the cakes are completely cool cover some of them in icing.

9. Decorate the others with blobs of icing, top with sweets of your choice, and serve!

Mwaaah haa-haa!

MOSHI TIP
If you want to make your Glump cakes look even more monstrous, then turn to make 65 and get designing your own fangtastic cupcake cases!

Billy Bob Baitman's Fishing Game

Let's hope you're better at fishing than Billy Bob Baitman! You might want to give him a few tips as the only thing he has caught lately is an old boot!

1. Draw round the plate on to your thick card and cut out the circle shape to form the base of your pond.

2. Tape a long strip of card around the edge to stop your fish from escaping, then decorate.

You Will Need

Plate
Thick card
Scissors
Ruler
Sticky tape
Felt-tip pens
Straws
String
Paper clips

3. Draw your fish and old boots on some more thick card, colour in both sides using felt-tip pens then cut them out.

4. Attach bent paper clips to each with sticky tape, to make the loops to hook your fish.

5. Make a fishing rod by tying a paper clip to the end of some string and shaping it into a hook. Tie the other end to a straw and secure with sticky tape.

MOSHI TIP
If you want to make lots of fish quickly, fold your card and cut out two or more fish at a time!

Foodies Sweetie Jars

Look at these goo-pendous jars. It's enough to give you the Moshi munchies! Just don't tell that sugary villain Sweet Tooth!

1. Cut a strip of white paper about half the height of your chosen jam jar. Make sure your jam jar is clean!

2. Concertina the strip of paper to make it look like a cake case. Wrap round the bottom of your jar and glue the ends.

3. Glue pompoms to the lid of the jar and glue a red pompom on top of these.

4. Finally, stick a length of ribbon around the rim of the lid and tie it in a bow. Your fangtastic jar is now ready to fill with sweets! Yummy!

5. Why not try wrapping your jars in coloured card or foam and decorating with pictures of sweets, coloured gems or foil?

You Will Need

Jam jar
White/coloured paper
Scissors
PVA glue
Ribbon
Pompoms
Sweeties

Try out different designs, using stick on gems, to make more moshitabulous sweetie jars.

Foodies Favour Cones

These zoomtastic cones are easy to make and look good enough to eat (but don't!).

You Will Need

Coloured card
White/coloured paper
Scissors
Plate
Pencil
PVA glue
Sweeties

1. Create a semicircle by carefully drawing round half a plate on to some coloured card.

2. Cut strips of coloured or white paper (approx 1cm wide). Then stick them to the semicircle at about a 45 degree angle.

3. Make the semicircle into a cone by folding around the edges.

4. Glue into place along the seam and hold while the glue dries.

Fill with sweeties and scoff!

Agony Ant Fortune Teller

We predict you'll be a monstrously good fortune teller with this easy-to-make little number . . .

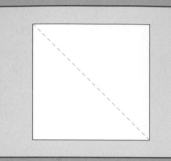

1. Take a square piece of paper and fold it in half to make a triangle. Then open it back up into a square.

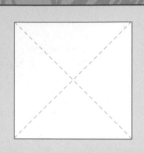

2. Fold the paper in half diagonally the other way to make a new triangle. When you open the paper this time, the folds should form an X.

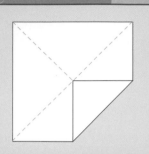

3. Fold all four corners towards the centre of the paper so the points meet in the middle.

Photocopy and cut out

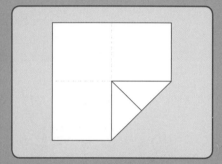

4. Flip the paper over so the folded side faces down. Now fold each corner on this side back towards the centre so the points meet in the middle to make a smaller square.

| MAIN STREET | Gift Island | OOH LA LANE | Bleurgh Beach |
| SLUDGE STREET | MUSIC ISLAND | THE PORT | FUN PARK |

5. On the same side, write Main St, Sludge St, Ooh La Lane, The Port, Gift Island, Music Island, Bleurgh Beach and Fun Park in each triangle or use the labels above.

6. Now open each flap and write a fortune on each of the triangles inside. Close each flap back up when you are done.

7. Flip the fortune teller over and draw a different Moshi on each of the four squares, or use the labels on the opposite page.

8. Fold the square vertically and then again horizontally to loosen it up. Now, you're ready to play!

Fortune Ideas:
1. Tomorrow is your lucky day.
2. Many Rox will come your way soon.
3. The number 9 will bring you good fortune.
4. Show someone how much you care with a hug.
5. Your Moshi friendship tree will grow bigger.
6. Check your garden for a new Moshling soon.
7. Try a new game at the Fun Park.
8. Simon says you'll be the next Underground Disco Champion.

KATS UMA

POP PET

How to use your fortune teller:
1. Put your index fingers and thumbs under the open flaps of the four sections of the fortune teller.
2. Have a friend choose one of the four monsters. Spell the monster's name out, while moving the fortune teller in and out.
3. Have your friend choose one of the places that is showing. Spell the place name out, while moving the fortune teller in and out as before.
4. Then have the person choose one of the four visible places. Open up the flap they choose, and read their fortune!

You Will Need

Paper
Scissors
Pen, pencil
Felt-tip pens

Photocopy and cut out

Flying Zoshlings Mobile

A monstrously mesmerising make! Boldly go where no Zoshling has gone before - your bedroom ceiling!

1. Ask an adult to cut your milk carton into flat pieces. Trace the Zoshlings on this page onto the pieces of carton, using glass paints. Colour them in, then leave them to dry.

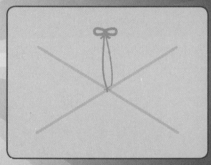

2. Make a cross with the chopsticks and secure them together in the middle with thread. Tie the ribbon around the middle and make a loop with it to hang your mobile up with.

3. Ask an adult to carefully cut out each Zoshling and make a small hole in the top of each one. Loop thread through the holes and tie a Zoshling to each end of the chopsticks.

Place your cut up pieces of plastic milk carton over these Zoshlings and trace away.

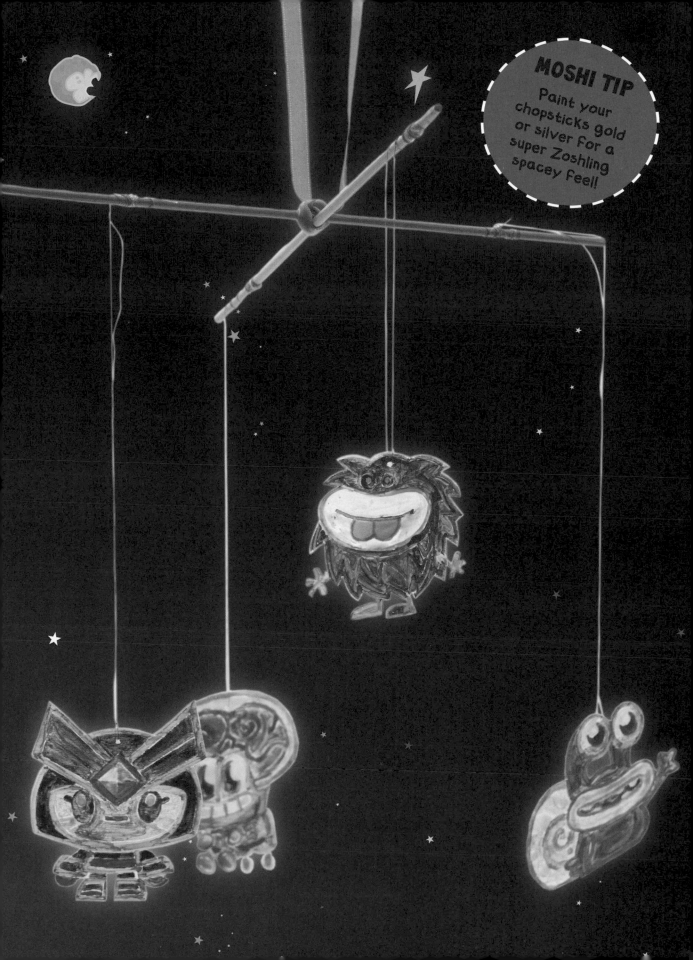

MOSHI TIP
Paint your chopsticks gold or silver for a super Zoshling spacey feel!

15 Felt Kitten of Good Fortune

Wave a paw and spread some mystic joy and happiness by making this purr-fect felt Tingaling . . .

1. Using the picture below as a guide, draw and cut out felt shapes to make Tingaling's head, ears and features.

2. Glue the shapes together to make Tingaling's face. Stick or sew on the white button eyes and her little bell.

3. Sew on extra details like her mouth and hair. Cut short lengths of ribbon to stick on as whiskers.

MOSHI TIP

You could make the felt Tingaling into a brooch or even stick it on the front of a birthday card!

You Will Need

Blue, white, black, pink and red felt
White ribbon
2 small white buttons
Bell
Needle and thread
PVA glue

Essence of Blue & Slug Slurp Slushie

These Moshi slushies are lushy! Gloopendous!

Essence of Blue

Makes 2 small glasses . . . or one big one!

You Will Need

300g/10oz blueberries
2 tbsp mild honey
250g/9oz vanilla
  yoghurt (approximately
  2 individual pots)
Extra berries or sweets
to decorate

1. Put your blueberries, honey and yoghurt into a blender. Ask an adult to help you whizz them up until the mixture is smooth.

2. Pour into your glass, decorate with extra berries or sweets (we used blue liquorice laces) and enjoy!

1. Put your kiwis and lime juice into a blender. Ask an adult to help you blitz until smooth.

2. Add your ice cream and blitz together again until fully combined.

3. Pour into your glass, decorate with jelly sweets and enjoy!

Slug Slurp Slushie

Makes 2 small glasses . . . or one big one!

You Will Need

250g/9oz Kiwis,
  peeled and quartered
Juice of half a small lime
150g/5½oz vanilla
  ice cream
Green jelly sweets to
  decorate

17 Glumps Bunting

Don't be grumpy, get Glumpy instead by stringing these blobs of badness up in your bedroom. Mwaaah haa-haa!

You Will Need

Small paper plates
Paint
Felt-tip pens
String
Masking tape
Craft materials
Assorted coloured card
Pencil

1. Pick which Glumps you're going to turn into bunting - there are twelve devious lumps to choose from! Paint a plate to look like each one.

2. You could draw any additional features like hair, eyes or mouths on a separate piece of card then stick them to your Glumps.

Print out or colour copy your Glumps' features to save time.

To make an even moustache, fold a piece of paper in half and cut out half a moustache, then open it up!

3. Stick string to the back of the top of the plates with masking tape. Leave a gap of about 20cm between each Glump.

4. Leave enough string at the end of the bunting to tie loops to hang your bunting from.

Music Island Instruments

The Moshi Monsters tom-toms are beating out a message to youuu! Make these monstrously easy drums to send a monsterific message of your own!

1. Paint your tub, or cover it in tissue paper in whatever colour you like.

2. Cut petal shapes from tissue paper to stick around the top edge of your tub.

3. Place your tub top down on a sheet of tissue paper and draw a wide circle around it. Cut out the circle and stick it to the top of your tub.

4. Crease the edges of the paper down round the sides of the tub. Cut out a circle of card to fit in the centre of the top of the tub, and stick it in place.

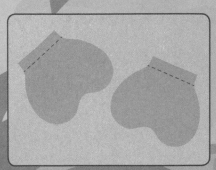

5. Cut out large leaf shapes from the card to stick round the bottom of your tub. Fold a little tab down on each leaf.

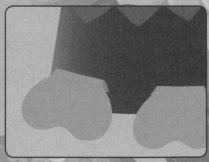

6. Put glue on the back of each tab, and press the tabs firmly down around the bottom edge of the tub.

You Will Need

Various sized plastic tubs
Tissue paper
Paint and paintbrush
Scissors
Coloured card
PVA glue

These leaves are heart-shaped, but you can make yours any shape you like.

Try tubs in different sizes to make different sounds!

MOSHI TIP

Concertina the paper for your petals and leaves so you can cut out a whole bunch at once!

Honey Bunny Carrot Cake

Honey and the other Funny Bunnies are always tucking in to a slice of carrot cake (or two) down in Pawberry Fields. Join them for a gossip and they'll swap this pawsome recipe with you!

MOSHI TIP

Cut out or trace the Bunnies on the opposite page, stick them on a cocktail stick and pop them on your cake!

Marzipan Carrots

Use a couple of drops of food colouring to make three quarters of your marzipan orange and the rest green. Divide the orange marzipan into four pieces and roll each piece into a carrot shape. Take the green marzipan and make two long leaves for each carrot. Now place the marzipan carrots on your finished cake as shown in the picture.

You Will Need

125g/4½oz self-raising
   flour
125g/4½oz plain flour
1 tsp bicarbonate
   of soda
2 tsp ground cinnamon
1 tsp ground ginger
250ml/9fl oz corn oil/
   vegetable oil
190g/6½oz soft
   brown sugar
4 eggs
175g/6oz golden syrup
400g/14oz grated
   carrot
60g/2oz chopped
   pecans
5 tbsp mild honey
23 cm/9 inch cake tin
Baking paper

To decorate

100g/3½oz unsalted
   butter, softened
2 tsp orange extract
100g/3½oz cream
   cheese
125g/4½oz icing
   sugar, sifted
Marzipan
Orange and green
   food colouring

1. Preheat the oven to 160°C/Gas Mark 3. Lightly grease a 23 cm/ 9 inch cake tin and line the base and sides with baking paper.

2. Sift the flours, bicarbonate of soda, cinnamon and ginger together in a bowl.

3. Whisk together the corn oil, sugar, eggs and syrup, and add to the flour mixture. Mix until fully combined, then stir in the grated carrot and nuts before spooning into the prepared tin.

4. Ask an adult to help you put the cake in the oven for 1 ¼–1½ hours until it is golden and springy to the touch.

5. Carefully remove the cake from the oven and, using a cocktail stick, make lots of holes over the top (pressing the stick in about half way through the cake). Slowly drizzle the honey over the top, leaving to cool for fifteen minutes before removing from the tin to fully cool on a rack.

6. To make the icing, beat together the butter, orange extract and cream cheese until light. Slowly add the icing sugar to the mixture until light and creamy.

7. Carefully slice the cooled cake in half and sandwich together with some of the icing, adding the rest to the top of your cake. Finish by decorating it with some marzipan carrots.

**20** # Pipe Cleaner Insects
Create an insect invasion with this little lot of creepy crawlies. Fang-tastic!

1. Using the ones on this page for inspiration, draw some monstrous Moshi insects onto corrugated cardboard, then cut them out.

You Will Need
Corrugated cardboard
Thin white card
PVA glue
Pipe cleaners
Paints and pens

2. Paint the corrugated card one colour, then add stripes or spots in different colours. Cut eyes and any other features out of paper and stick them in place.

3. Cut the pipe cleaners into equal lengths for each insect's legs. Slot them into the gaps in the edges of the corrugated cardboard.

4. Your gang of creepy crawlies is now ready! Time to have some monsterific fun!

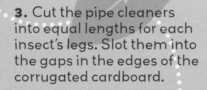

Princess Ponies Winning Rosettes

These stunning rosettes are fit for horsey royalty. One-trick ponies? More like pirouetting Princess Ponies!

1. Fold a sheet of A4 paper into a concertina (each strip should be 3cm). Fold in half and tie some thread round the centre.

2. Glue the two open ends together to create a semi-circle. Repeat step 1 to make another semi-circle and stick the two halves together to create the rosette.

3. Stick a circle of coloured card in the centre.

You Will Need

Different coloured paper
Scissors
Ruler
Pencil
PVA glue
Sticky tape

Try a different design on each rosette you make. This one's a circle covered with a tissue paper collage.

To make this rosette, cut out a circle and trace round it on a new piece of paper. Draw petals around the new circle, cut this out and stick the two together.

MOSHI TIP

Measure your folds carefully for award-winning results.

This stripe design was made by drawing lines on the paper before folding it. What can you come up with?

Rocky Stone Slab Doorstop

Prop your bedroom door open with this stony-faced, heavy-weight hunk of Baby Blockhead!

1. Take your large box and stuff it full of scrunched-up newspaper. Tape the top shut.

2. Tape the four smaller boxes to the large box to form Rocky's nose, ears and the bump on top of his head.

3. Paint the whole head with PVA glue. Lay strips of toilet paper over the box to create a 'rocky' surface. Leave to dry.

4. Once the head is rock hard, paint it and allow to dry again.

You Will Need

1 large rectangular box
4 small rectangular boxes
Newspaper
Sticky tape
Scissors
Paintbrush
PVA glue
Toilet paper
Paints
Pencil
Felt-tip pens

5. Using a pencil, mark out where the eyes and mouth are going to go.

6. Paint Rocky's eyes and teeth with white paint and allow to dry.

7. Use coloured paints or felt-tip pens to add the remaining details to his face, as shown in the picture.

8. For the finishing touch, add 'cracks' to Rocky's head with a felt-tip pen.

Why not use a pencil to carve into your Baby Blockhead before the toilet paper is completely dry, to add extra craggy details?

Blurp's Gloop

Make your own slimy monsterific Gloop!

You Will Need

A mixing bowl
Cornflour
A tablespoon
A jug of water
Food colouring (we chose green)
A mixing spoon

1. Add five or six heaped spoonfuls of cornflour to your clean bowl.

2. Fill your jug with cold water from the tap, then add a few drops of food colouring. Just a little is perfect, it's powerful stuff!

3. Make a well in the middle of your cornflour and pour a little of the coloured water in it. Start to slowly mix the water and cornflour together with your spoon. Don't mix too fast or it won't work.

4. Once the water and cornflour are really well combined, add a little more water to the bowl and mix slowly again. Keep doing this until your mixture feels just like Gloop.

5. Gently tap the surface of your Gloop with a spoon. If it's made properly, your spoon should bounce off the surface as if you were hitting rubber.

6. Now here's the clever bit. Stir it again and it should still feel like a liquid. Neat, huh?!

MOSHI TIP

Don't worry if it gets too watery, just sprinkle in a little more cornflour until you get the consistency you're after. If you've never handled Gloop before, it feels just like custard!

For your first batch, start small. So about two tablespoons of cornflour should do it. As you become an experienced Gloop producer you can use more.

Make a Pack of Cards

Creating your very own set of Moshi playing cards is goopendously easy. Just copy the designs below . . .

You Will Need

Card
Scissors
Use of a photocopier
Crayons/Colouring
pencils/Felt-tip pens

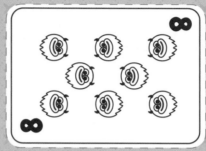
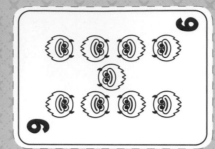
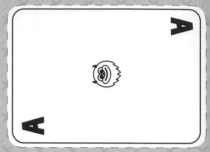

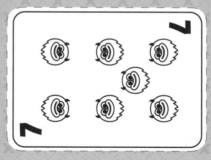

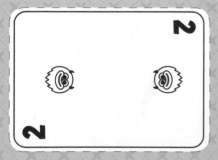

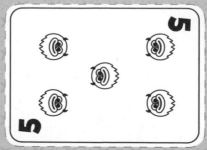
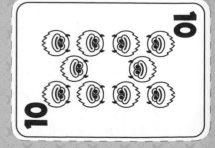

Photocopy or trace the set of cards on this page four times. Colour each set of thirteen cards in a different colour to make a complete pack of fifty-two cards. You're now ready to play Moshi Monsters card games with your furry friends.

Dodgy Dealz Card Trick

Pull the furry wool over your friends' eyes like that tentacled trickster, Sly Chance, with this simple, but oh so impressive trick . . .

1. Lay the cards out in this order: 6, 5, 4, 3, 2, A, J, 10, 9, 8, 7 (A is the Ace and J is the Joker) face down on a table.

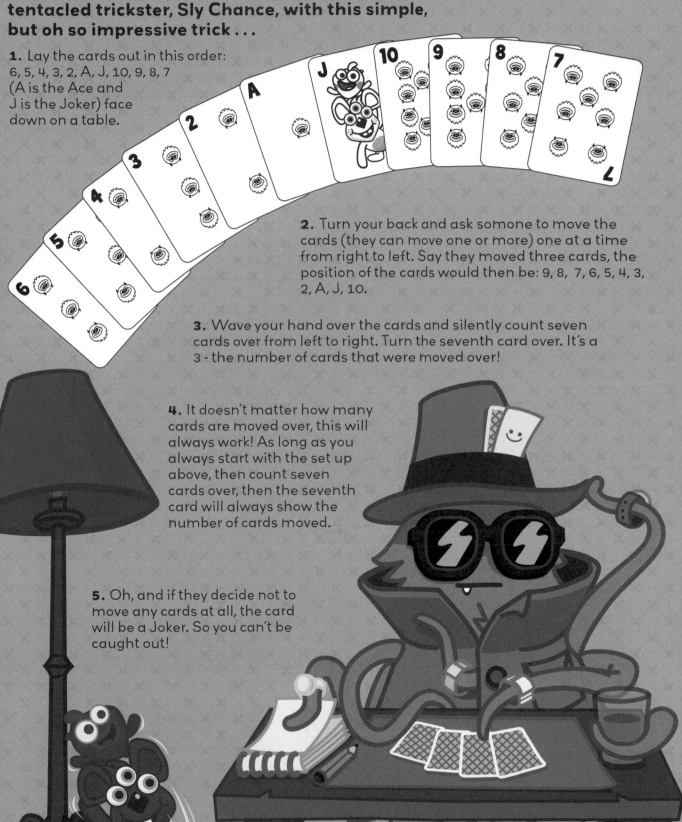

2. Turn your back and ask somone to move the cards (they can move one or more) one at a time from right to left. Say they moved three cards, the position of the cards would then be: 9, 8, 7, 6, 5, 4, 3, 2, A, J, 10.

3. Wave your hand over the cards and silently count seven cards over from left to right. Turn the seventh card over. It's a 3 - the number of cards that were moved over!

4. It doesn't matter how many cards are moved over, this will always work! As long as you always start with the set up above, then count seven cards over, then the seventh card will always show the number of cards moved.

5. Oh, and if they decide not to move any cards at all, the card will be a Joker. So you can't be caught out!

25

Roarsome Cheesecake

Roarberry Cheesecake is a monstrous Moshi Monster delicacy, but our tasty version doesn't bite back!

1. Make sure you have a 20 cm/8 inch loose-bottom tin for this recipe. Put the biscuits into a freezer bag, seal it shut and crush them with a rolling pin until they look like breadcrumbs. Pour them into a bowl.

2. Carefully add your melted butter to the biscuits and mix well. Pour the biscuit mixture into your tin and press it down to make a firm base. Put the tin in the fridge while you make the filling.

3. Prepare the gelatine using the instructions on the packet and leave to one side. In a separate bowl whisk your cream until it forms soft peaks.

4. In a large bowl, mix the melted chocolate, cream cheese, orange zest and orange essence until smooth. Add 3tbsp of your prepared gelatine and mix well. Fold the whipped cream into this and mix carefully until fully combined.

5. Remove the tin from the fridge, pour the filling on top of the biscuit base and return the tin to the fridge to set for one hour.

6. After an hour you can make your orange jelly using the instructions on the packet. You only need 285ml/½ pint of jelly for this recipe. Leave your jelly to come to room temperature, remove your cheesecake from the fridge and carefully pour your jelly mixture on top before returning the tin to the fridge until the jelly is set.

Once your jelly is firm, carefully remove the cheesecake from the tin, decorate with your tinned orange segments and serve.

You Will Need

Base:
100g/3½oz gingernut biscuits, crushed
120g/4oz Digestive biscuits, crushed
100g/3½oz butter, melted
20 cm/ 8 inch loose-bottom tin

Filling:
11g/⅓oz gelatine (or Vegi-Gel)
375ml/12½fl oz double cream
250g/9oz white chocolate, melted
400g/14oz cream cheese
Zest of 1 orange
1 tsp orange essence
Orange jelly cubes or powder, to make 300ml/½ pint
Tin of orange segments

Tyra's Spa Face Mask

Down at Tyra's Spa, the glitzy fashionista recommends that you try wearing your yogurt instead of eating it! It might make your fur a little sticky, but it makes a fab moisturiser . . .

1. Mix together your yogurt, orange juice and zest.

2. Wash your face before applying the mask.

3. Apply the mask to your skin a little at a time, taking care to avoid your eyes.

4. Leave for twenty minutes before rinsing off with lukewarm water.

You Will Need

2 tbsp plain yogurt
Juice and zest of ½ of an orange
(make sure you wash the orange
first and ask an adult to help you
with the zesting!)

MOSHI TIP
These masks are pretty messy, so ask a grown-up to help you and make sure you clear up afterwards!

Tyra's Spa Face Mask

Use these labels for your bottles and containers.

MOSHI TIP
Keep your face and hair masks in the fridge and use within three days.

27 Tyra's Spa Hair Mask

Want shiny, silky hair like the goopendous Tyra Fangs'? This oaty recipe will do the trick . . .

1. Mix the oil, oatmeal and milk together well. Add the mashed banana until fully combined.

2. Give your hair a good brush, then apply a golfball-sized blob of the mixture to your hair, avoiding your eyes.

3. Massage in, leave for twenty minutes, and relax.

4. Wash your hair thoroughly to remove all traces of the hair mask.

5. Shampoo, dry and admire your luscious locks! Fangtastic!

You Will Need

2 tsp olive oil
2 tbsp oatmeal
1 tbsp milk
1 small banana, well mashed

Tyra's Garbage Day Perfume

Don't chuck this in the bin – it smells monstrously divine!

1. Take your bowl and place the cheesecloth inside, leaving the edges hanging over the bowl.

2. Put the flowers in the bowl on top of the cheesecloth, and then pour the water over them.

3. Cover the bowl with a tea towel and let it sit overnight.

4. The next day, using the edges of your cheesecloth, pull it out of the bowl.

5. Gently squeeze the scented water from the cheesecloth into the small pan.

6. Simmer the water until about one teaspoon is left. Ask an adult to help you with this.

7. Cool and place in a small bottle. Your perfume will have a shelf-life of about one month.

8. Dab on to your neck and wrists and wait for the compliments! Moshitabulous!

You Will Need

I cup water
I cup freshly chopped
Flower blossoms
   (try lavender, lilac,
   orange blossoms, roses
   or even honeysuckle)
Bowl
Cheesecloth
Small pan
Small bottle

You will need to go through this process a number of times to fill a bottle!

Use this label for your bottle.

Tyra's SPA
Garbage Day Perfume

Tyra's SPA
Face Mask

Tyra's SPA
Garbage Day Perfume

Tyra's SPA
Hair Mask

29

Hansel Psycho Gingerboys

Crumbs! These are so gloopendously delish you'll need a candy cane to ward off naughty cookie thieves . . .

1. Preheat your oven to 190°C/Gas Mark 5 and lightly grease two baking trays.

2. In a bowl, sift together the flour, baking powder and ground ginger. Using your fingertips rub in the butter until the mixture looks like breadcrumbs.

3. Stir in the sugar. Make a well in the centre of your mixture and add the egg and treacle.

4. Stir together until the mixture forms a dough. If a little dry, add the milk. On a floured surface give your dough a little knead for two minutes.

5. Flour your surface again and roll out the dough until 5 mm/$\frac{1}{5}$ inch thick.

6. Cut out your Gingerboys using a cutter and place them on the baking trays. Make sure they're evenly spaced as they spread when baked.

7. Bake in the oven (get an adult to help you with using the oven) for eight to ten minutes until they're light brown. Cool on the trays for two minutes before putting them on to a wire rack.

You Will Need

350g/12oz plain flour
2 tsp baking powder
2 tsp ground ginger
100g/3½oz chilled butter, diced
175g/6oz soft brown sugar
1 egg, beaten
115g/4oz treacle
1 tbsp milk (optional)
Gingerbread man cutter
Baking trays

To decorate:
Coloured icing tubes (we used
   black and white)
Some jelly beans for the buttons

Makes approximately 20 Gingerboys,
   depending on the size you want.

Once completely cool,
use your coloured icing
tubes to decorate
your Gingerboys.

Make sure you give your
Gingerboys eyes, mouths and
some colourful jelly-bean
buttons. You can use a little
of the icing to stick these on.

Gift Peppy

Peppy's head is normally filled with thoughts of engine oil and fish heads, but you can put anything in your pongy Peppy . . .

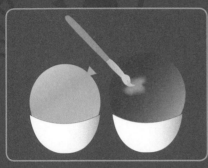

1. Blow up your balloons, one slightly more than the other and stand each in a small dish. Paint with PVA glue.

2. Cover two-thirds of each one with a layer of newspaper and allow to dry.

3. Add a further six layers to each balloon, allowing each to dry between applications.

4. Coat the final layer with PVA glue, allow to dry, then pop your balloons by sticking a pin in each one.

You Will Need

2 balloons
Paintbrush
PVA glue
Newspaper
Scissors
Paints
Red, yellow and white card
Blue shiny card
Red ribbon

5. Cut the larger ball two-thirds of the way down to make a bowl shape. Cut the smaller ball just where it starts to curve under to make a smaller bowl shape.

6. Mix PVA glue and white paint together to create a base coat. Cover the bowls with the mixture and leave to dry.

7. Paint the bigger bowl black. This will form Peppy's hat.

8. Make Peppy's nose with yellow card, using the templates below. Score the dotted lines to fold the card into a beak shape. Glue in position.

9. Paint all of the smaller bowl white, apart from the beak. Leave to dry then paint the back of it black.

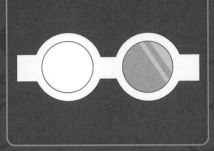

10. When everything's dry, place the black hat bowl on top of the white head bowl, and paint on eyes and dotty cheeks.

11. Cut Peppy's glasses out of red card, plus two round disks out of blue shiny card for the lenses. Glue in the lenses.

12. Attach the the red ribbon to the glasses and make sure this fits around the hat. Glue everything in place.

Photocopy or trace this template on to white card. Cut out the skull and crossbones to stick on the front of Peppy's hat.

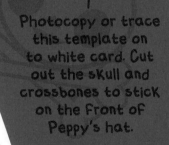

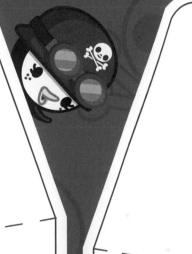

Photocopy or trace the beak templates onto yellow card. Cut along the solid lines and fold along the dotted lines.

Gift Island Wrapping Paper

'Tis always the season to send prezzies wrapped up and tagged with this fangtastic little lot. Why not get Clutch to deliver them for you?

You Will Need

Sheets of paper
Paint
Knife
Scissors
A potato
A piece of sponge
Felt-tip pen
Hole punch
Ribbon, string or
    pipe cleaners

1. Get an adult to help you cut a potato in half, then draw your shape on the flat surface of the potato.

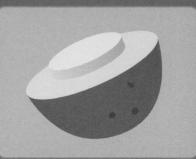

2. Ask an adult to cut around the shape you have drawn with a knife, removing any excess potato so that the shape is raised.

MOSHI TIP
Turn to activity 86 to find out how to make gift bags!

3. For the sponges, draw your shape on the sponge with a felt-tip pen. Then cut around the shape with scissors.

4. Use different colours of paint and make a pattern printing with the potatoes and sponges. Evenly spaced patterns work with bright colours. Why not try printing on brightly coloured papers, too?

32 Gift Tags

Special delivery from Skeeter Rydell – monsterific gift tags for all your furry friends' prezzies!

Cut your paper to the size and shape you would like your gift tag to be. Decorate with potato or sponge prints and then hole punch the corner. Use ribbon, string or pipe cleaners to complete the tags.

Add glitter or sequins to your tags for extra sparkle!

Knitting Stitches

1. Tuck the purple needle through the first loop – it should lie behind the red one.

2. Wrap the trailing wool round the purple needle from right to left.

3. Push the purple needle through the hole between the trailing wool and the stitch. Bring the purple needle back up to the front.

4. Slip the stitch off the red needle, keeping it on the purple one.

5. Repeat as necessary until you have the length of stitches required.

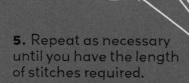

Casting Off

1. Knit two stitches then insert the tip of the left needle into the first stitch on the right needle.

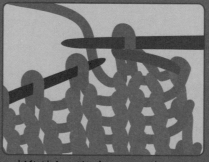

2. Lift this stitch up and over the second stitch and off the right needle.

3. To cast off the next stitch, knit one more stitch and repeat step 1. Continue until one stitch remains.

4. Cut the wool leaving a 20cm tail. Pass the end of the wool through the last stitch and pull tight. Sew the tail into the knitting to finish.

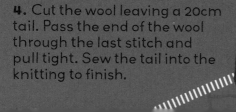

Spamburger

For a fangtastically messy, but gloriously tasty monster feast, make these gloopendous little Spamburgers!

You Will Need

1 red onion, chopped
1 tbsp olive oil
1 tin Spam (340g/12oz)
1 tsp mixed dried herbs
1 egg, lightly beaten
2 tbsp plain flour
Extra flour for
    shaping

4 small burger buns
Lettuce
Tomatoes, sliced
Mayonnaise

Makes 4 small burgers

1. Ask an adult to help you chop and fry your onion in the olive oil until soft. Remove from the heat and leave the onion to cool completely.

2. In a large bowl, use your hands to break up the Spam, then mix in your herbs, cooled onions, beaten egg and flour until fully combined. Use your hands to make four small burgers, dipping them in the extra flour if the mix becomes sticky. Chill the burgers in the fridge for one hour.

3. Ask an adult to help you fry your burgers in a pan on a medium heat with a little oil. Cook them on each side for about five minutes or until they start turning light brown.

4. Once cooked, put your burgers into your buns and top with lettuce, tomatoes and mayonnaise. Now you can gobble them up!

Decorate with an eyeball to make your spamburger really monstrous! We made our eye with a ball of icing painted with food colouring!

35 Cap'n Buck's Pirate Hat

Ahoy there, me hearties! A swashbuckling hat that looks a million pieces of eight!

You Will Need

Large sheets of black paper
White paint
Pirate stencil (see make 83)
Sticky tape

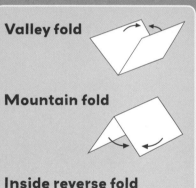

Valley fold

Mountain fold

Inside reverse fold

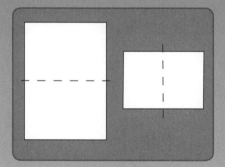

1. Fold a piece of black paper in half, then in half again. Open out the second fold.

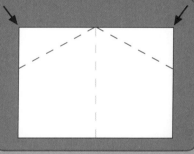

2. Fold the corners in as shown by the dotted lines, then fold them back the opposite way. Take the corners indicated by the arrows and push them inside the piece of paper to make an inside reverse fold.

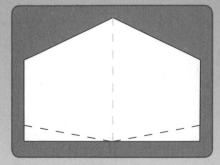

3. Make valley folds as shown above on the top layer of paper. Turn over and repeat the valley folds on the other side.

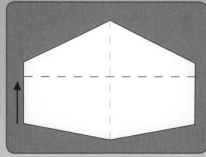

4. Fold the paper below the dotted line upwards, again on both sides of the paper.

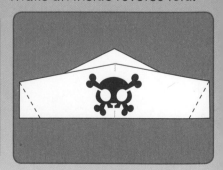

5. Make a small mountain fold on either side of your hat and secure the corners in place with sticky tape to complete your pirate hat.

Cap'n Buck's Pirate Boat

Anchors away! Make your own Moshi pirate vessel!

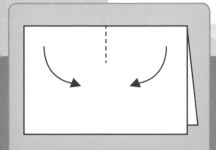

1. Begin with a rectangular piece of paper. Fold it in half, then partially fold it again, making a crease near the top.

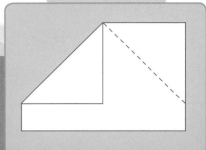

2. Fold down the corners as shown above.

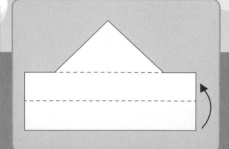

3. Now fold the edges of the paper upwards as shown on both sides. Use your fingers to open up into a hat shape.

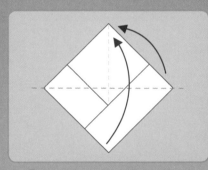

4. Bring the corners of the hat brim towards each other and flatten it down into a square.

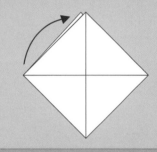

5. Take the open corners of the square and fold each one upwards to create a flattened triangle.

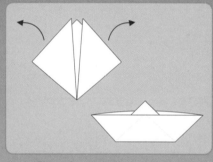

6. Gently pull the sides of the triangle outwards and flatten to make a boat shape. Open it out slightly to complete your boat. Stencil on a skull and crossbones.

Furnando's Magic Pictures

Abracadabra and presto chango, these magic pictures will have you amazed and astounded.

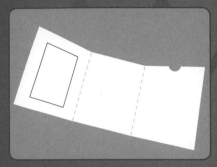

You Will Need

Thin card or paper
Scissors
Felt-tip pens/crayons
Sticky tape
Plastic Folder
Marker pen
Glitter

1. Fold a sheet of thin card into three equal sections. On the front flap draw a rectangle. Cut out the finger grip space as shown in the picture with step 2.

2. Open the folded card out again and cut out the rectangle that you drew on the front flap. Decorate the frame round the rectangle-shaped hole.

3. Cut a separate piece of paper the same size as the front of the card. Draw on your design, using felt-tip pens.

4. Slip your picture into a plastic folder with the top against a fold. Trim the plastic to fit. Stick the back of the picture to the plastic.

5. Use a marker pen to draw an outline of the picture on to the plastic. Get the card frame you made in steps 1 and 2, and open it out flat.

6. Fold the bottom flap into the middle. Slip the plastic-covered picture over the bottom flap. The bottom flap is now between the coloured picture and the outlined picture on the plastic flap. Fold the top flap over the plastic and stick in place.

Now for the magic! Grip the plastic and paper and pull; the picture will appear in colour as you pull it out. **Magic!**

3-D Moshi Badges

Make yourself a monstrously good badge. You'll look fangtastic!

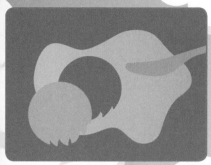

1. Roll out clay in the colour of your chosen Moshi and cut out the shape required.

2. Use other colours to make the mouth and eyes. You can use a long, thin sausge of clay to add depth to the outline too, as shown in the pictures. Then leave your design to dry.

3. Finally, varnish your badge for a goopendously shiny effect. Glue on the brooch back and wear with monster pride!

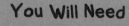

You Will Need

Clay in a variety of colours
Modelling tool
Varnish
Brooch backs
PVA glue

Pop-up Cards

Make your very own Moshitabulous pop-up cards and dazzle your friends and family. You don't need a reason to send a card!

1. Fold your card in half to form the outside of your card.

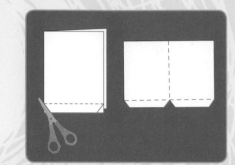

2. Now take another smaller piece of card and fold in half. Make the tabs to stick it in place by folding up 1cm from the bottom and cutting off the corners as shown. This is your pop-up.

You Will Need

Coloured thin card
Scissors
PVA glue
Coloured paper
Felt-tip pens

Decorate your pop-up with your favourite Monsters, scenes and presents. Whatever you fancy . . . get creative!

MOSHI TIP
Why not make lots of different pop-up cards? Turn the page to see some more designs . . .

Don't forget to design the front of your card. Write your message with felt-tip pens.

3. You need to make sure the positioning of your pop-up will be correct. Position it on the inside of the larger piece of card and draw lines to indicate where you are going to stick it.

4. Draw or collage your design on to the smaller piece of card, then glue the tabs to the guidelines you have drawn.

These pops are deceptively simple – measure out each storey, cut them out and glue them in place before going to town with the detail.

Experiment with making your cards different shapes and sizes.

ShiShi Tissue Box Cover

Wrap your tissue box up in this pretty pink fur, ready for any Sneezing Panda emergency.

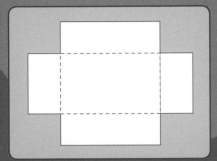

1. Using your tissue box as a template, measure out the above pattern on your fur material.

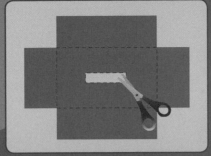

2. Cut the pattern out, using scissors, then cut a rectangular hole in the middle to pull the tissues through.

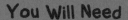

You Will Need

Tissue box
Ruler
Pencil/Pen
Furry fabric
PVA glue
Scissors
Card
ShiShi cut out

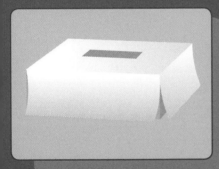

3. Place the cut out fur over your tissue box with the fur side down. Make sure the hole in the fabric is above the hole in the box, to access your tissues.

4. Cut four small pieces of card the same height as your box. Fold them around each corner of the box and glue them to the inside of the fur to create your cover. Slide the cover off the box and turn it fur side out.

5. Stick your ShiShi cut-out on to the top of the cover and slide it over your tissue box.

Trace around me, colour and then cut out to decorate your tissue box.

I.G.G.Y. T-shirt

Give your drab old tee a monstrous makeover. It's better than a tickly pickle.

1. Trace or draw your design on to your T-shirt with a soft pencil.

2. Use fabric paints to carefully fill in the image.

3. Leave it twenty-four hours for the paints to dry. Ask an adult to carefully iron according to the fabric paint instructions to seal your design.

Trace this I.G.G.Y. as a template.

You Will Need

T-Shirt
Pencil
Fabric paints
Iron

MOSHI TIP

Use puffy fabric paints for a 3-D effect on your design.

42 Pompom Boomer

Well Squiddly Dee, here's how to make your own fluffy Boomer!

1. Using your compass, trace out two circles, 8cm in diameter. Draw a smaller circle, 5cm in diameter, in the middle.

2. Now cut out both larger circles, then cut out the inner circles. Place the two card circles together.

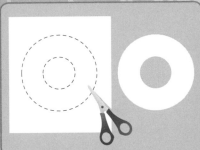

You Will Need

Cardboard
Scissors
Compass
Wool
Ribbon
Black, yellow, red felt
PVA glue

3. Cut the wool into manageable lengths. Wrap the wool around the card circles as shown below. Keep repeating until there is no space left to wrap any more wool through the holes.

4. When your rings are full, cut the wool around the edges. Your scissors should eventually pass through the two pieces of cardboard.

5. Pass a length of wool between the two pieces of cardboard, around the wool and tie firmly in a knot to secure all your wool pieces together. Pull the card circles out of your pompom and discard. Trim any lengths of wool that are uneven to make your pompom perfectly round.

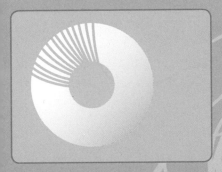

Add some black felt eyes, yellow felt cheeks and a happy red felt smile. Tie some ribbon twice round your pom pom. And boom! A fluffy Boomer!

Swirlberry Muffins

No need for a trip to the Gross-ery Store when you can rustle up these Moshitabulous muffins from the comfort of your very own kitchen. Gloopendous!

You Will Need

175g/6oz butter
1 tsp vanilla extract
175g/6oz caster sugar
3 eggs
175g/6oz self-raising flour
125g/4½ blueberries, washed
Twelve hole muffin tin
Muffin cases

For the Icing:

50g/1¾oz butter
125g/4½oz cream cheese
Juice and zest of ½ lemon
300g/10½oz icing sugar, sifted
A couple of drops of blue food colouring
Blueberries to decorate

Makes 12 muffins

1. Preheat the oven to 190°C/Gas Mark 5 and pop your paper cases into a twelve hole muffin tin.

2. Cream together the butter, vanilla extract and sugar until light and fluffy. Beat in your eggs one at a time with a little of your measured flour until fully mixed.

3. Fold in the remaining flour using a metal spoon, and once combined mix in your blueberries.

Don't go mad with the food colouring, a few drops will go a long way.

4. Evenly distribute the mixture between the muffin cases and bake in the oven (get an adult to help you) for fifteen to twenty minutes until risen and firm to the touch. Remove the tin from the oven, remove the muffins from the tin and leave them to cool on a wire rack.

5. To make your icing, beat together your butter, cream cheese, lemon zest and juice until just combined. Add your icing sugar and beat until light and fluffy. Add a couple of drops of blue food colouring and beat together until the mixture is a blueberry colour.

6. When your muffins are completely cool, decorate them with the cream-cheese icing, top each with blueberries and serve!

Scrumpy's Frame

Make this splat-tastic frame to showcase your own monsterpieces or photos of you and your friends.

1. Use a photo or some of your artwork to work out how large the frame should be. Cut out the frame shape from a piece of thick card.

2. Use the string to create a swirly pattern or any other pattern you desire, on the frame. Glue the string in place and leave it to dry.

3. Using scissors, cut out squares of your tissue paper, in as many different colours as you want.

4. Spread the card frame with glue and gently press the squares of tissue paper over the frame. Tuck the edges in, carefully smoothing the tissue paper for a neat finish.

5. Add your photo and attach with sticky tape on the back.

You Will Need

Thick Card
Ruler
Pencil
Scissors
String
PVA glue
Coloured tissue
  paper
Sticky tape

45 Rox Twistmas Tree

Bring some bling and sparkle to your Twistmas festivities with this Rox tree!

1. In order to make a cone for your Christmas tree, follow the instructions from make 12.

2. Stick ribbon around the tree to decorate. Now glue on jewels to make it sparkle like a real Christmas tree.

3. Photocopy, then cut out Roxy, or trace her and place on top of your Rox Christmas Tree.

You Will Need

Thick green card
Large plate
Pencil
Ruler
Scissors
PVA glue/sticky tape
Jewel Rox and ribbon
   to decorate
Roxy cut-out

Felt Beanbag Cleo

Make your own Pretty Pyramid . . .

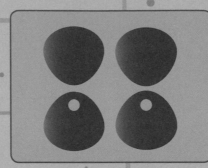

1. Draw the star shape opposite on to yellow felt and then cut it out. Also cut out two arms from black felt.

2. Now cut out four feet from the purple felt (two pieces to make each foot). Cut a small slit in the top of two of the foot pieces.

3. Cut four small slits on the yellow felt as indicated on the template opposite.

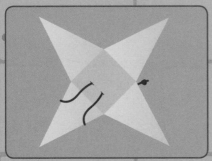

4. Take two lengths of black cord (10cm each) and tie a knot in one end of each. Feed the other end through each slit in the base to form the legs.

5. Push the arms through the slits on either side, gluing them into position on the inside. Turn the shape over and draw on a brick pattern with a felt-tip pen, leaving space for Cleo's face.

6. Stitch on cheeks and a smile with pink thread. Cut out eyes from the remaining black felt and glue in place. Use the purple ribbon to make a small bow and set to one side.

7. Thread the foot pieces with holes on to the black cord. Knot the cords at equal lengths and cut off any excess. Now glue the remaining foot pieces to the bottom of Cleo's feet to hide the knots.

8. Sew the sides of the pyramid together to form your pretty Cleo. Before you finish sewing the final side, fill her with lentils. Now add the finishing touches by sticking on the cute little bow!

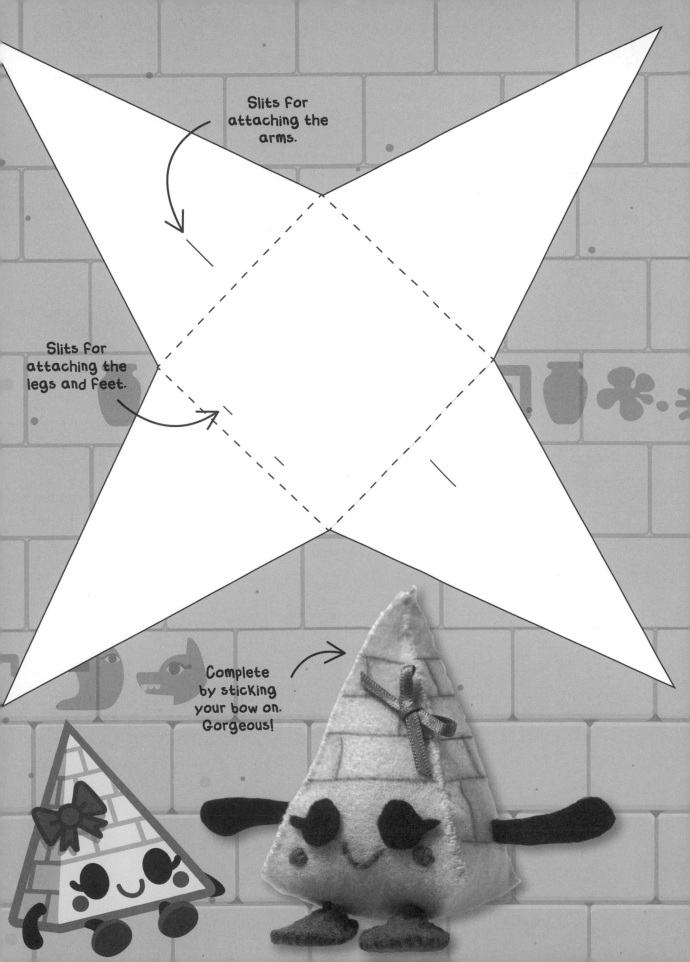

Slits for attaching the arms.

Slits for attaching the legs and feet.

Complete by sticking your bow on. Gorgeous!

47 Clutch Lettercards

Make these fun lettercards to fold up and send to your friends. Clutch loves making special deliveries!

You Will Need

White paper
Plate
Colouring pencils
Paints
Ruler
Pencil
Stickers
Scissors

1. Trace around a large plate on to a piece of white paper. Now cut it out using your scissors.

2. Draw a small rectangle in the centre of the circle using a pencil and your ruler. Leaving the rectangle shape clear, paint or colour a pattern on to the rest of your circle.

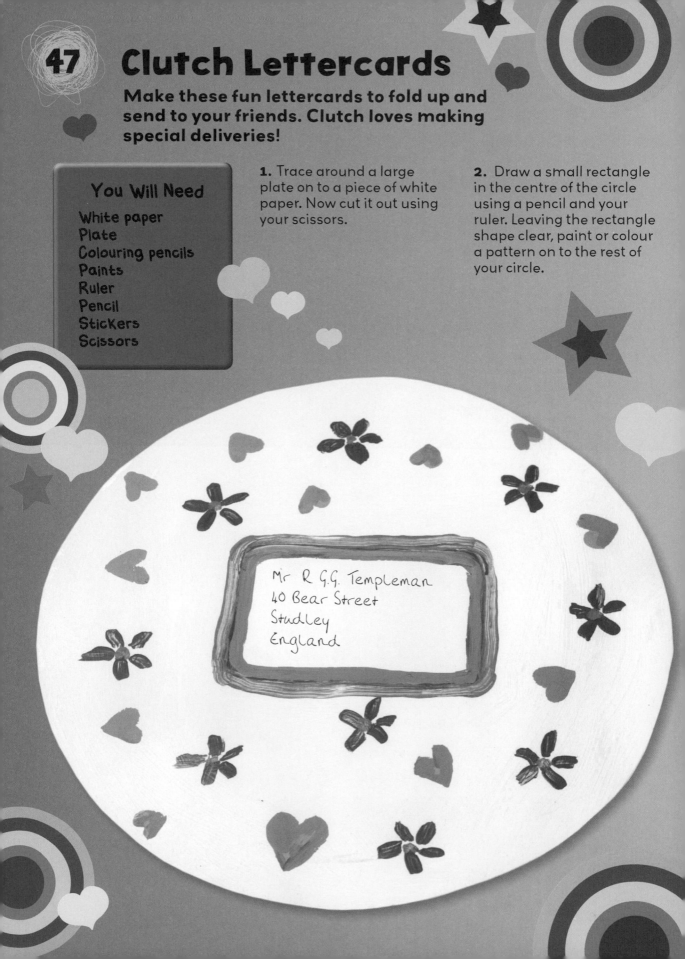

Mr R G.G. Templeman
40 Bear Street
Studley
England

Use glitter paints or pens if you have them for extra sparkle.

Miss Emma M. Alphabet
Flat b, 116 London Road
Clarm
England

3. Turn your lettercard over and draw lines using a pencil and a ruler. These lines are to help you write your message neatly on your lettercard.

Granny Smith
Two Cottages
Little Windley
England

4. When you've written your letter, fold in all four sides and hold in place with a sticker. Don't forget to add a stamp before mailing!

McNulty's Code Wheel

Psst . . . guess what? You can be an Undercover Yap Yap with this super secretive code wheel. Pawsome!

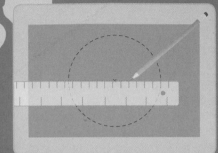

You Will Need

Thin card
Paints & paintbrushes
Compass & protractor
Scissors
Ruler
Pencils & felt-tip pens
Split pin

1. Take a piece of thin card and draw a circle on it with your compass. Mark the centre and draw a line through the middle. Cut the circle out.

2. Place a protractor on the centre line and mark at twelve degree points round the top half of the circle. Turn it upside down and mark the rest of the circle in the same way.

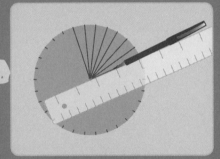

3. Now take a ruler and draw a line from the centre of the circle to each of the marks. Then make another larger disc in exactly the same way.

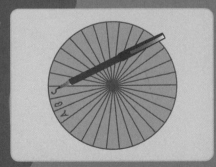

4. On the big circle write the numbers 1–30 in each gap. In the small circle write the letters A–Z and in the four remaining spaces write 'no', 'yes', a full stop and leave one blank.

5. Punch a hole through the middle of both circles. Join them together with a split pin. Now you just need to decorate it.

Setting the Code

1. To make the code wheel work, the person you are sending coded messages to will have to have the same code wheel, too.

2. Choose a letter and number to set your code on and make sure you tell your friend what it will be. On this wheel, the code is set on 5 and A, so 5 equals the letter A.

3. Write a message using the numbers around the edge that correspond to the letters and punctuation in the centre of the wheel.

4. You will now have a message written entirely in numbers for your friend to decode!

Example:
29 19 25 / 12 5 26 9 / 7 22 5 7 15 9 8 / 13 24

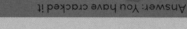

Answer: You have cracked it

Fifi Hair Clip

Make this funky hair frippery – it's fit for a snooty Oochie Poochie!

1. Cut out a cloud shape from some white felt and glue it to a hairclip.

2. Glue a heart-shaped gem over a glitter heart and stick it to the felt. Wear with pride and give that fashionista pooch a run for her Rox!

You Will Need

Plain hair clips
White felt
Glue
Heart-shaped gems
Glitter heart
PVA glue

MOSHI TIP

Use a ready-made glitter heart from a craft shop.

Make Your Own Newspaper

Get on down to *The Daily Growl* Offices and join that all-seeing roving reporter Roary Scrawl - it's your monster chance to make front-page news!

1. Create your very own hot off the press edition of *The Daily Growl* on the pages below, or use them as a guide to draw your own newspaper on paper.

2. Decide what you're going to write your articles about and put the headlines in the grey boxes. Why not interview family or friends for your story?

3. Illustrate your writing with either your own drawings or photographs, or cut out pictures from old magazines and newspapers.

Moshlings Paper Garlands

Get snippy making these easy-peasy paper chains. You could even throw a Moshi Monsters party afterwards as an excuse to show off your handiwork!

You Will Need
Thin coloured paper
Scissors
Sticky tape
Felt-tip pens
White paint
Paintbrush

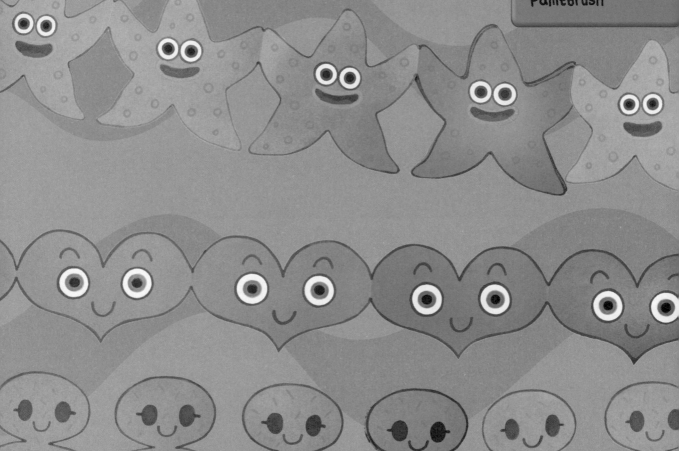

1. Concertina your paper, joining sheets together with sticky tape to make a long chain.

2. Draw the outline of your chosen Moshlings on the top sheet of the concertina, then cut round it.

3. Open out the concertina and bring your paper garland Moshlings to life using your felt-tip pens and white paint.

MOSHI TIP
Instead of painting on the eyes, why not use round white stickers to save time?

We used Hansel, Tiamo and Fumble for our garlands, but Monstro City is your oyster!

ClueKoo Bird Feeder

Squawk! Make this feeder and you might attract some Birdy Moshlings to your garden. Look, up in the sky . . .

You Will Need

Empty/clean milk or juice carton
Scissors
Paint
Paintbrush
Strong tape
String
Wild bird seed or fat balls

1. Ask an adult to help you cut away a large rectangle shape in each of the four sides (as shown in the picture). Leave a thicker border at the bottom of the carton to hold the bird seed.

2. Paint your bird feeder in Cluekoo colours and leave to dry.

3. Attach a piece of strong tape in a loop to the top of the feeder. Fill the bottom with bird seed or fat balls.

4. Hang your bird seeder in a safe place in your garden, out of the reach of cats.

You can always thread some peanuts on a piece of string and hang it up next to the feeder.

Beanie Blob Canvas

Add some colour to your room by creating your very own beautiful blobby work of art! Googenheim Gallery, here you come!

You Will Need

A canvas
Felt-tip pens
Buttons
Felt
Foam
Scissors
PVA glue

1. Paint your canvas the colour you wish and leave it to dry. (Watching paint dry is really boring, so go do something else instead.)

2. Draw out your Beanie Blob shapes on the foam and cut them out.

3. Glue the blob shapes on to your canvas.

4. Use scraps of foam, buttons and pieces of felt to create the faces and hair of your Beanie Blobs. Hang your canvas on your wall, then sit back and admire your work!

Poppet Friendship Bracelets

When it comes to dressing up, fashion-forward Poppet is a Moshi on a mission. Just take a look at these cute friendship bracelets.

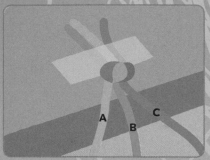

1. Choose three lengths of different coloured threads. Make a knot at one end to hold the threads together. Tape the knot end to your work surface.

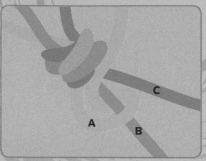

2. Hold thread B with your left hand. Take thread A around B and push it through the loop to make a knot and pull the thread.

You Will Need

Selection of coloured thread
Sticky tape
Scissors
Table or work surface
Friends to give your bracelets too (unless you decide to keep them yourself!)

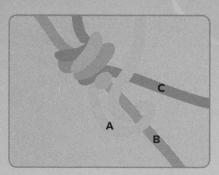

3. Do the same thing again. You should have two knots on thread B.

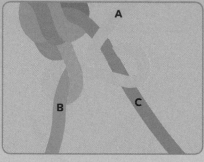

4. Hold thread C with your left hand. Take thread A around C and through the loop to make a knot, pull the thread and then do it again.

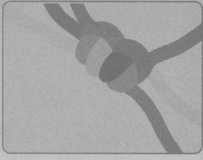

5. Now start the next row. Make knots from left to right. Knot B twice on to C, then twice on to A. For the third row, knot C twice on to A, then twice on to B.

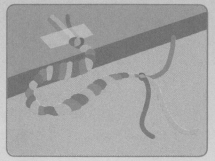

6. Keep knotting the threads in rows until you have made a braid long enough to go round your wrist. Tie the loose ends in place with a knot.

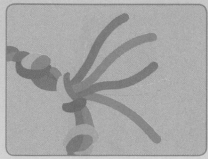

7. Your fangtastic BPF (best Poppet friend!) bracelet is now complete. Make a double knot at each end and trim away any extra thread.

Thread beads on to your bracelets before you tie the double knot to secure them. Why not stitch gems and sequins on them to give them a super-cute Poppet touch?

Glump Juggling Balls

No doubt about it, Dr. Strangeglove's evil minions make excellent juggling balls . . .

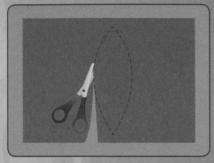

1. Cut six pieces of fabric using the pattern template on the opposite page.

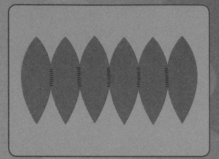

2. Stitch the shapes together in a row as shown.

You Will Need

Coloured Fabric
Thread
Needle
Coloured Felt
Scissors
Lentils

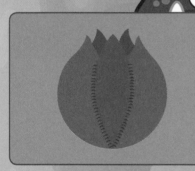

3. Close up one end of the ball by stitching the pointed ends together. Stitch down the remaining side, but leave a gap open at the top.

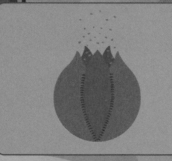

4. Turn inside out to hide the seams and fill with lentils. Stitch the gap closed at the top of the ball.

5. Decorate by sticking felt shapes on to the ball to make it resemble whichever Glumps you have chosen. Mwaaah haa-haa!

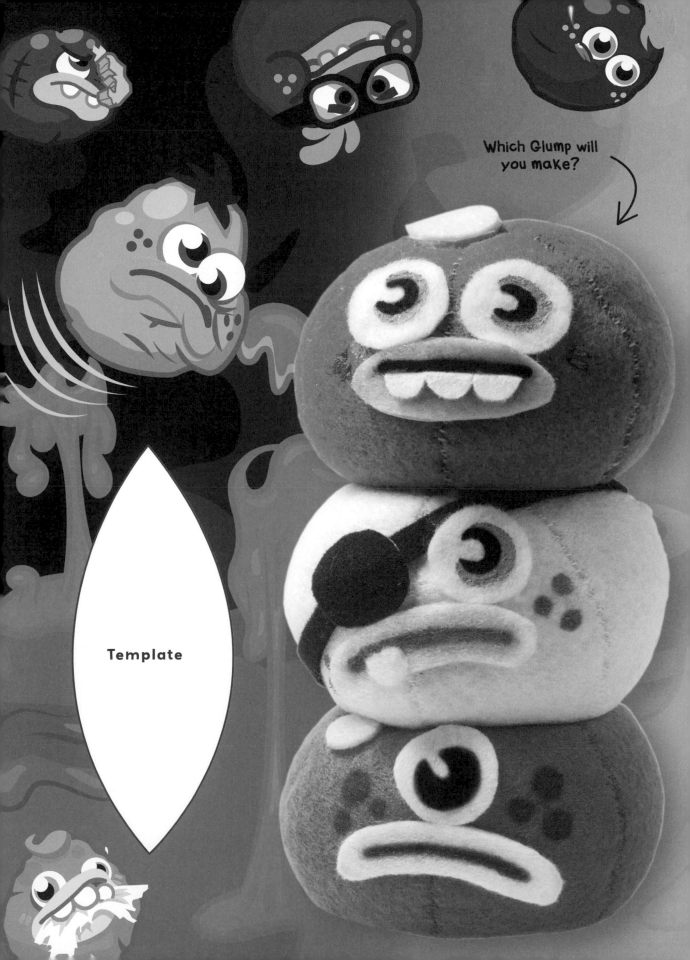

Which Glump will you make?

Template

Mini Ben Clock

Clong! Making your own Teeny TickTock is easy. Read on to find out how . . .

1. Draw around the clock face with a pen on to your card. Then sketch out Mini Ben's outline around it.

2. Cut out your Mini Ben and then use the scissors to punch a hole through the clock face circle, then carefully cut it out.

You Will Need

An old clock
Felt-tips
Paints and paintbrushes
Thick card
Scissors
Felt or Foam to decorate
String
Pompoms

3. Decorate Mini Ben and add his eyes using paints or felt-tip pens. Add a big ol' felt moustache and eyebrows too!

4. Cut our arms and legs from thick card or foam. Glue them to the back of the card, then glue the clock to the back of Mini Ben too, so that the clock face is visible through the hole.

Bong! Bong!

5. Paint string and glue it around the edges of the clock tower to add detail. Stick a mini pompom to the top of the tower, then attach a loop of string to the back to hang your Mini Ben from.

If your old clock has a hook on the back of it use it to hang your new Mini Ben.

Colonel Catcher's Flutterbies

Help the flutterby catcher catch these gorgeous beauties as they flutter by . . .

1. Cut out lots of little flutterbies in different types of paper and material.

2. Create a landscape using layers of tissue paper glued on to your piece of card.

You Will Need

Craft materials
PVA glue
Tissue paper
Card
Colour copy of Colonel Catcher
Scissors
Felt-tip and glitter pens

3. Use felt-tip or glitter pens to add bodies and details to your flutterbies.

4. Colour photocopy or trace the picture of Colonel Catcher, then cut him out and stick him on your picture. Finally, glue your flutterbies around him and see how many he can catch!

Clay Moshling Zoo

Make your very own clawsomely cute clay Moshling models and build a zoo to keep them in. It's Moshling-tastic!

1. To make DJ Quack, soften and mould the yellow clay into the shapes above with your hands.

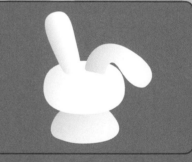

2. Attach DJ Quack's head to his body by pressing down firmly and make sure his body has a good base so he can stand up.

1. To make Honey, mould the white clay into the shapes above.

2. Stick Honey's head on to her body, and make sure her body has a good base so she can stand up.

3. Add Honey's ears to the top of her head, making sure one is bent over.

Turn the page to make a zoo for your Moshlings.

1. To make Lady Meowford, soften and mould the white and purple clay into the shapes above.

2. Make a firm base with her feet, then add her body and head on top. Then add her ears and tail.

Oven bake clay –
yellow, red,
black, white and
purple
A rolling pin

Modelling tool
Oven tray
Green paper
and card
Scissors

Sticky tape
Red tape
Shoebox

MOSHLING ZOO

3. Next, secure DJ Quack's feathers and beak to his head and his wings and legs to his body.

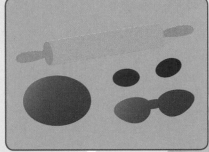

4. Roll out the red and black clay, then cut out the shapes for Quack's sunglasses and belly.

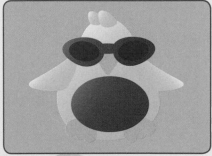

5. When you are happy with your final model, place it on an oven tray and ask an adult to bake, as per the clay baking instructions.

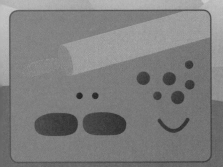

4. Roll out and attach two purple blobs for Honey's feet. Add red spots to her dress and give her a big happy smile.

5. Add two black circles for eyes, then place her on an oven tray and ask an adult to bake, as per the clay baking instructions.

3. Roll out the purple clay and cut out two circles and eyelashes as shown.

4. Add the purple part of her eyes then stick two white circles of clay over them. Add two more white circles to her dress for paws.

5. Finally, add two black circles to her eyes, then another two white dots on each eye, as shown, then ask an adult to place it in the oven as above.

Moshling Zoo

1. Discarding the lid, cover the inside of a shoebox in green paper. Use red tape to reinforce the corners.

2. Cut out two shelves from a piece of green card. Bend over the ends and secure them inside the box (as shown in the picture) with sticky tape.

3. Make a 'Moshling Zoo' sign out of white card and attach it to the top of the box. Now you can place your clay Moshlings inside! Moshlingtastic!

59 Cali Headband

Make yourself this gorgeous headband and see if you can sense any romance . . .

You Will Need

Hairband
Ribbon
Beads and
   jewels for
   decoration
PVA glue

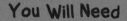

1. Wrap your headband in your chosen ribbon and glue down at the ends.

2. Once the glue is dried, decorate the headband with jewels and beads and large hearts. Glue them into place and allow to dry.

Moshling Garden Plant Pots

How does your garden grow?
In a Moshi pot, of course!

1. Paint your pots with a base coat. Make sure you completely cover the pot. Leave to dry then apply another coat of paint.

2. Once dry, decorate with patterns or Moshlings, then pop in a plant!

Choose your favourite plants or flowers to go in your fangtastic pots. Or you could grow herbs, fruits or vegetables in them!

Tamara Tesla's Tangram

This amazing puzzle will keep you entertained for hours!

You Will Need
Square pieces of card
   or paper
Scissors
Ruler
Pencil

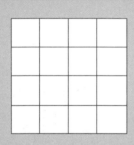

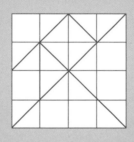

1. Fold the square paper in half, then in half again. Repeat this step. Unfold the paper.

2. Using the fold lines as a guide, draw red lines on your square as shown above. Take your scissors and cut along these red lines.

3. You will now have seven pieces. Make more sets of shapes on different coloured card by following steps 1 to 4 again.

4. You can arrange these seven pieces into an incredible number of shapes – even Moshlings. See how many you can create using all your different coloured shapes!

Think about your Moshis' features: eyes, mouths, wings and so on. Cut them out of card to add to your puzzle.

Kissy Pen Tops

This pencil topper is cute as a Baby Ghost! Woo-ooh-ooh!

1. Using the picture as a guide, cut out two head shapes from white felt.

You Will Need

White Felt
Pencil
Blue pipe cleaner
Pink Felt
Pink ribbon
Black Felt-tip pen
Scissors
PVA glue

4. Make a bow from pink ribbon to stick to the top of her head. Cut her mouth and cheeks from pink felt and glue them in place. Finally, draw on her black eyes.

2. Twist a blue pipe cleaner around the top half of a pencil, leaving a straight tail piece at the top.

3. Place the tail of the pipe cleaner in-between the two felt head shapes and glue them all together.

Buster's Scrapbook

It's your Moshling expert-in-residence, Buster Bumblechops, here to show you how to make the most splendiferous travel book ever. Moshlingtastic!

1. Cut up different coloured papers and materials to create a monstrous collage design for your scrapbook cover. Glue all the pieces of your picture on to a sheet of paper. Be as wild and creative as possible with your design!

You Will Need

Collage items and lots of bits of paper
2 pieces of thick card
Felt-tip pens and pencils
Scissors
PVA glue
Hole punch
Wooden chopstick
Sandpaper
Plain elastic hairband

You could cut pictures and individual letters out of magazines and newspapers to embellish your scrapbook cover design.

2. Design and cut out your title lettering and stick this on to your picture. Glue this cover picture to one of the pieces of thick card, and trim to fit.

3. Hole punch the front cover card, the back cover card, and lots of sheets of paper, all in the same place. Easy-peasy-gooberry-squeezy!

4. Pull the hairband through the holes so the ends stick out of the front cover. Slip the chopstick through both ends of the band. This will securely bind the scrapbook cover and pages together.

Wheelie YumYum Cakes

Woo-Woo! Make way for some delightfully delicious cupcakes! Goopendously yummy!

1. Preheat the oven to 190°C/Gas Mark 5 and pop your paper cases into a twelve hole muffin tin.

2. Cream together the butter, almond extract, vanilla extract and sugar until light and fluffy. Beat in your eggs one at a time with a little of your measured flour until fully mixed.

3. Fold in the remaining flour using a metal spoon and mix in your chopped cherries.

4. Evenly distribute the mixture between the muffin cases and bake in the oven (get an adult to help you) for fifteen to twenty minutes until risen and firm to the touch. Remove the tin from the oven, remove the muffins from the tin and leave them to cool on a wire rack.

You Will Need

175g/6oz butter
½ tsp almond extract
½ tsp vanilla extract
175g/6oz caster sugar
3 eggs
175g/6oz self-raising flour
12 glacé cherries chopped
Muffin tin
Muffin cases

Makes 12 cupcakes

5. To make your icing, beat together your butter, cream cheese and vanilla extract until smoothly combined. Add your icing sugar and beat until light and fluffy.

6. When your muffins are completely cool, decorate them with the icing, top each with a glacé cherry and sprinkle with hundreds and thousands.

Icing

50g/1¾ oz butter
125g/4½ oz cream cheese
1 tsp vanilla extract
300g/10oz icing sugar, sifted
Some glacé cherries and hundreds and thousands to decorate

MOSHI TIP

Use the cake case template on the next page to make these Wheelie YumYum cases.

Cupcake Cases

Moshify your cupcakes to the max with these cool decorative cases.

You Will Need

Thin card
Scissors
Crayons or
Felt-tip pens

Trace over this template on to thin card. Design and colour your own cupcake case. Then cut out each strip and fold the ends round to meet each other. Insert the tab end into the slit at the other end. Place your fangtastic case around your scrumptious cupcakes!

Cut this slit open with your scissors so that you can insert the tab at the other end of the strip of card.

Photocopy (or trace and colour) these Glump design cupcake cases for make 9.

Mwaaah haa-haa!

Glump-a-licious!

Blingo's Blinging Jewellery

These slick and funky beads are totally dazzling, just right for Blingo The Flashy Fox's jewellery collection.

You Will Need

Air-hardening clay
Kebab skewers
Bowl (to lie the beads
    across while they dry)
Paintbrush
Paint
Water-soluble varnish
Black ribbon

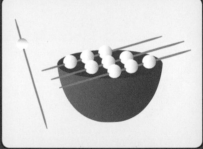

1. Make balls of clay. They can be small or chunky, it's up to you.

2. Push a skewer through the middle of each ball, wiggling it a bit to create a good-sized hole. Lie the skewers across the bowl and leave the beads to go hard.

3. Leave the beads on the skewers while you paint, then varnish them.

4. Remove beads from skewers and thread through ribbon to make necklaces or bracelets.

It's all about the price tag baby. Make square beads and decorate with dollar signs. Ker-ching!

Shape some clay into a star and twinkle away.

Red and gold beads make a super-bling bracelet.

Froggie Doggie Door Hanger

Knock, knock! Who's there? Ribbit! It's a dog who thinks he's a frog... pawsome! Or should that be flipper-tastic?

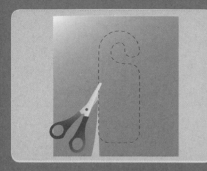

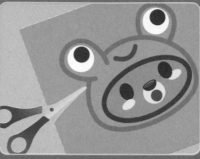

1. Cut out a rectangular piece of foam with a hook shape at the top (to go over your door handle) to form your hanger.

2. Draw and cut out your foam letters, then draw a picture of a Froggie Doggie on your coloured paper and cut it out. Alternatively, you could photocopy the picture of Scamp on this page and cut that out instead.

You Will Need

Coloured foam pieces
Scissors
Coloured paper
Glue
Pink pipe cleaner
Scissors

3. Glue everything in place and add a pipe cleaner bow as the finishing touch!

Write 'Do Not Disturb' on your hanger handle if you want to keep out unwanted guests!

SAM'S ROOM

Prof. Purple×Bookmark

Make this birdy boffin bookmark. It's better than a big brain pie with extra brain sprinkles. Just take care that it doesn't scoff your book. Burp!

You Will Need

Thin card
Pencil
Crayons or felt-tip pens
Scissors

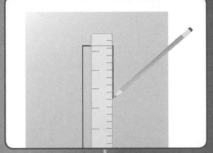

1. Draw a long rectangle with a ruler, big enough to use as a bookmark.

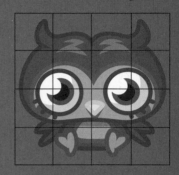

Use as a template to draw the Prof.

2. Now draw Prof. Purplex sitting at the top of the rectangle. When you're happy with your design, cut your bookmark out.

3. Use felt tips or crayons to colour in your picture and add as much detail as you can.

TOP TIP

Why not create more bookmarks using your other favourite Moshlings?

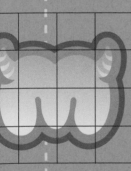

Peppy the Stunt Penguin Kite

Feeling the need for speed? This is great to fly (in-between scoffing pilchard popsicles, of course!).

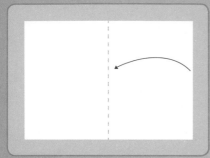

1. Start with your A3 piece of paper. Fold it in half. Mark a point on the top and the bottom of the paper about five inches from the fold.

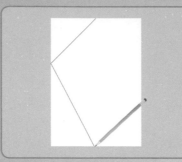

2. Mark a point about four inches from the top on the open side. Draw a line connecting the dots and cut along the lines.

You Will Need

A3 paper
2 kebab skewers
Crêpe paper
Piece of coloured card
Kite string
Pencil
Scissors
Paints, felt-tip pens
  and crayons
Sticky tape
Hole punch

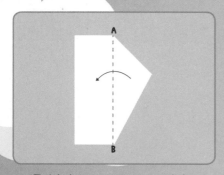

3. Fold the top corner of the paper along the top point A to the bottom point B.

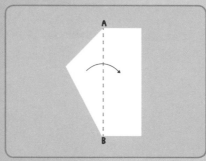

4. Now flip the paper over and fold the other side down to match the side you've just folded.

5. Open up the kite and decorate it. Let your imagination go wild. Make it ROARSOME!

6. Put a piece of sticky tape on the top corner of each wing. Use your hole punch to make a hole in each wing on the area where the sticky tape is. Tie your kite string through these holes.

7. Tie an overhand loop knot (as shown in the picture) exactly in the centre of the string to make the bridle. (The bridle is how the line you fly the kite with attaches to the kite.) Make sure you tie a good tight knot!

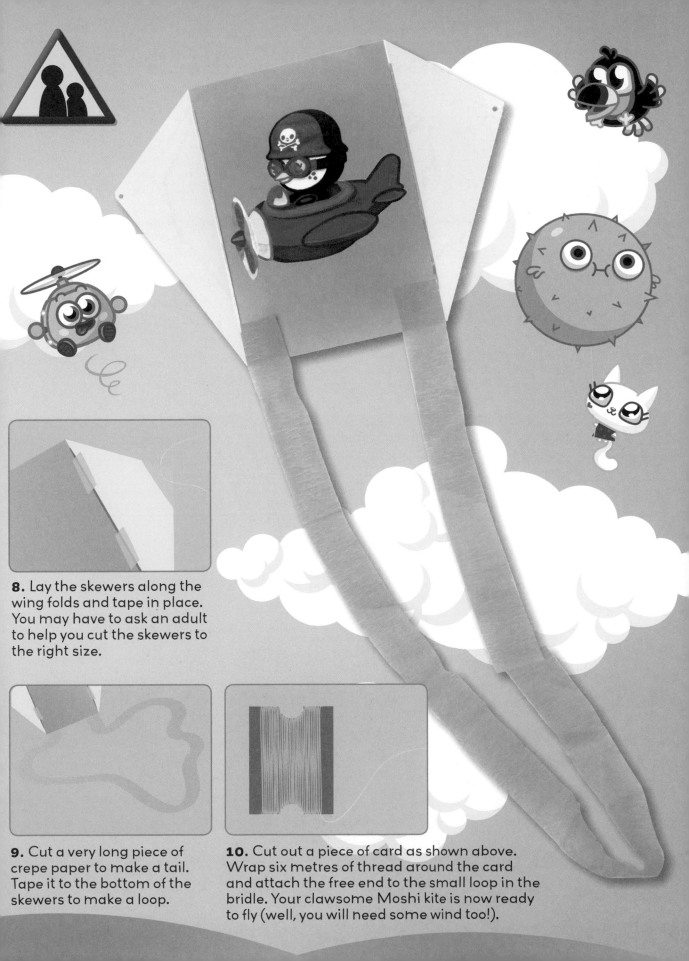

8. Lay the skewers along the wing folds and tape in place. You may have to ask an adult to help you cut the skewers to the right size.

9. Cut a very long piece of crepe paper to make a tail. Tape it to the bottom of the skewers to make a loop.

10. Cut out a piece of card as shown above. Wrap six metres of thread around the card and attach the free end to the small loop in the bridle. Your clawsome Moshi kite is now ready to fly (well, you will need some wind too!).

Big Bad Bill's Pumpkin Carving

Making this fur-raising flickering face is easier than saying 'Umba-wanga-thlunk'!

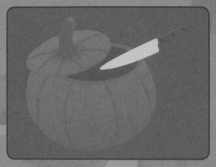

1. Ask an adult to chop off the top of the pumpkin.

2. Now gouge out the insides.

You Will Need

Pumpkin
Knife
Spoon
Pen
Candle
Matches/lighter

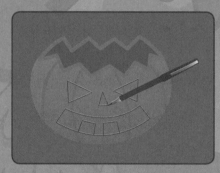

3. Draw a face with jagged teeth on to the side of the pumpkin.

4. Ask an adult to cut out the eyes, nose and mouth. Add an eyepatch or other interesting details if you like!

5. Place a candle inside, ask an adult to carefuly light it and pop the lid back on. Spooky!

MOSHI TIP
You could use the pumpkin seeds to make teeth for your scary carving!

MOSHI TIP

You don't have to stick to pumpkins. Why not try a spooky watermelon head instead?

71

Moshi Mug

It's Moshi drinkin' time. Check out this ROARSOME make. Smokin'!

You Will Need

Plain mug
Pencil and paper
Ceramic paints
Paintbrushes

1. Make sure your mug is clean before you start. Draw your favourite Moshi or Moshling on to your mug.

2. Now fill in your design with ceramic paints. Leave it to dry while you catch some ZZZZZs overnight.

3. Ask an adult to fix the colours by 'baking' your mug in an oven. (Make sure you follow the ceramic paint manufacturer's instructions.)

MOSHI TIP

Initial and date your work of art on the bottom of your mug. It could be worth a lot of Rox one day!

Spookies Silhouette Picture

Woo-ooh! Give any passer-by the w-o-b-b-e-r-l-y willies with these creepy creations!

You Will Need

2 pieces of black card
Coloured tissue paper
Pencil
Scissors
Sticky tape

1. Draw a creepy picture on to black card and cut it out.

2. Stick different coloured tissue papers with tape to the other piece of card, leaving a border all around the edges to form a picture frame.

3. Finally, stick your black silhouette picture on top of the tissue paper. Scare-tastic!

MOSHI TIP

Make more spooky silhouettes with any spooky character.

Mr. Snoodle Container

Make the sleepiest, snuffliest storage container around!

You Will Need

- Container with lid
- Scissors
- Newspaper
- Cardboard tube
- PVA glue
- Paint
- Paintbrushes
- White paper
- Felt-tip pens

1. Tear up pieces of newspaper and glue them on to your container to create a good painting surface.

2. Cut slits around one end of your cardboard tube, fan them out, and glue it to the side of your container to create his snout. Glue paper over the other end of the tube.

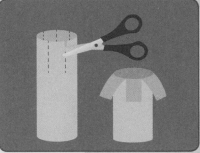

3. When dry, paint on your base colour then add Mr. Snoodle's spots.

4. On a piece of paper, draw, colour in, and cut out his ears and eyes, then glue them in place.

5. Use your super snuffly container to store your Moshi treasures!

Humphrey Sock Puppet

Quit lollygagging around and make your own Snoring Hickopotumus.

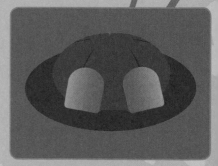

This puppet will really sock it to them!

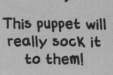

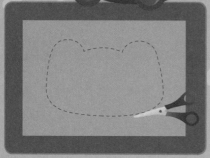

1. Cut the muzzle shape out of card. Draw round it on to blue felt and cut this out. Push the card cut-out to the base of the grey sock. Stick the blue felt in place on top of the sock foot.

2. Cut out two black felt eye shapes, and two dark blue felt ovals for the nostrils. Now cut a white felt oval for the mouth. Stick them in position as shown above.

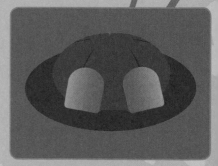

3. Now make the hat. Use the templates opposite to cut out the base and dome of the hat from brown card.

4. Fold the tabs of the dome under and glue the edges to the base of the hat to create the dome.

5. Cut out the ear shapes (as shown) from grey card. Fold a tab at the bottom of each ear and glue them on to the front of the hat by pushing each tab under the dome. Put the sock on your hand and glue the hat in place.

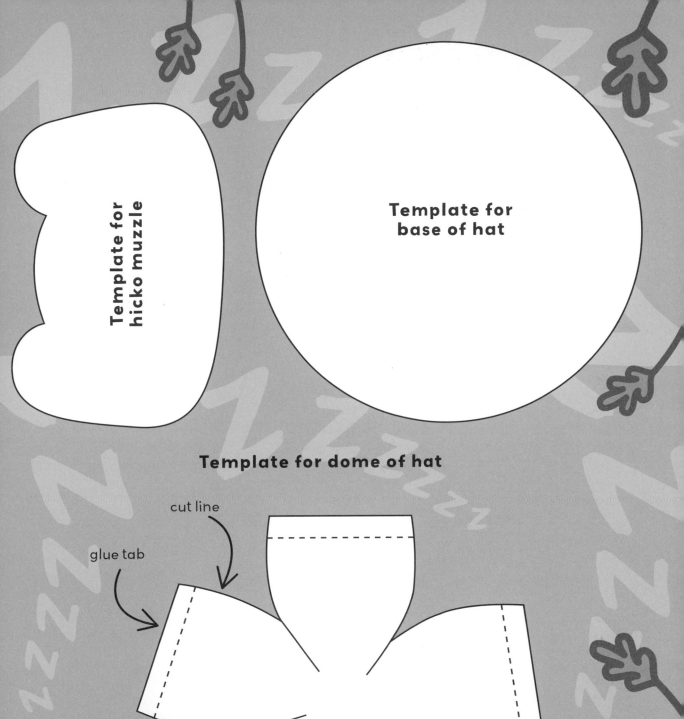

Template for hicko muzzle

Template for base of hat

Template for dome of hat

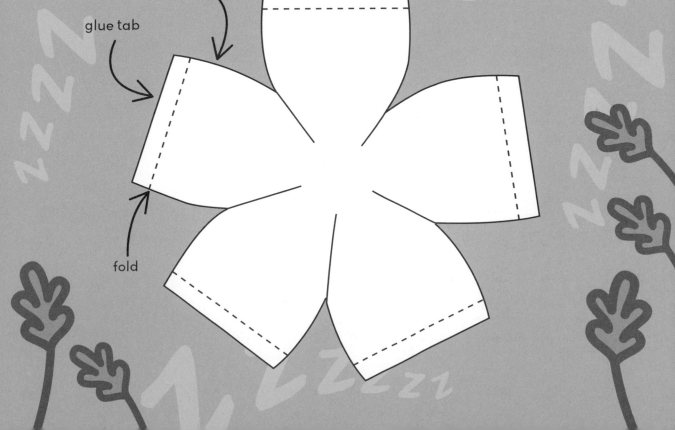

cut line

glue tab

fold

Pooky Cress

Make this playful Potty Pipsqueak. The extra cress will help protect him from any passing Killer Canaries!

You Will Need

Eggs and egg box
Cotton wool
Cress seeds
Acrylic paint
Cardboard tube
Craft Knife
Green tissue paper
PVA glue

1. Cut a short length from the cardboard tube and wrap the tissue paper around it, tucking the edges into the ends.

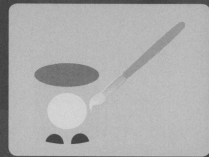

2. Now paint on some green spots for Pooky's tummy and two dark green semicircles for the feet. This is the body for your egg head to rest on.

MOSHI TIP

Keep the seeds damp so they sprout.

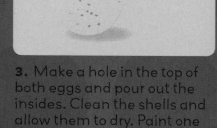

3. Make a hole in the top of both eggs and pour out the insides. Clean the shells and allow them to dry. Paint one shell green and leave it to dry.

4. Now cut the top off the other shell. Make it as jagged as you like. Paint it white and add the zig-zag crack detail.

5. Paint Pooky's face on to the green shell, then gently press damp cotton wool inside it and sprinkle a few cress seeds on top.

4. Put the white egg shell over the head shell and place them on the tube body. Leave Pooky somewhere light and watch the seeds grow through the hole in his hat!

Moshi Spoon Heads

Going stir crazy? Follow these instructions and you'll spoon be having the time of your life . . . !

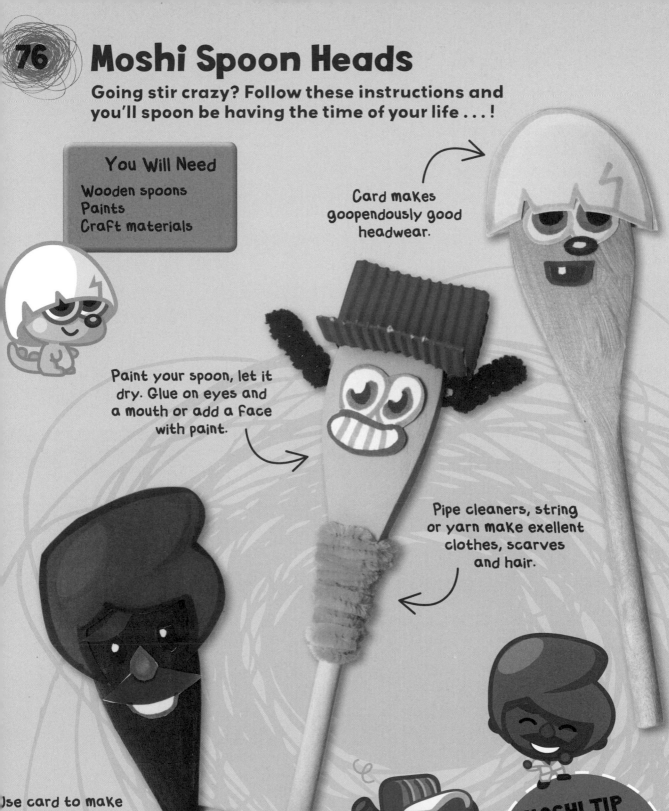

You Will Need

Wooden spoons
Paints
Craft materials

Card makes goopendously good headwear.

Paint your spoon, let it dry. Glue on eyes and a mouth or add a face with paint.

Pipe cleaners, string or yarn make exellent clothes, scarves and hair.

Use card to make a collar that is truly spoontacular!

MOSHI TIP

If you don't have a wooden spoon, use permanent pens to draw on a plastic one.

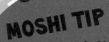

DJ Quack Specs

You'll be strutting your monster stuff like a Disco Duckie at the Underground Disco in these super stylish specs.

You Will Need

Paper and card
(in various colours)
Craft Knife
Scissors
Pencil
Sketching Paper

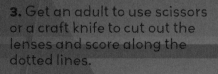

1. Photocopy or trace the glasses template onto your chosen colour of card.

2. Cut around the template.

3. Get an adult to use scissors or a craft knife to cut out the lenses and score along the dotted lines.

4. Draw some boogie-tastic ideas of the design you want to make, then copy your design on to your chosen materials and get sticking!

Fold along the dotted line

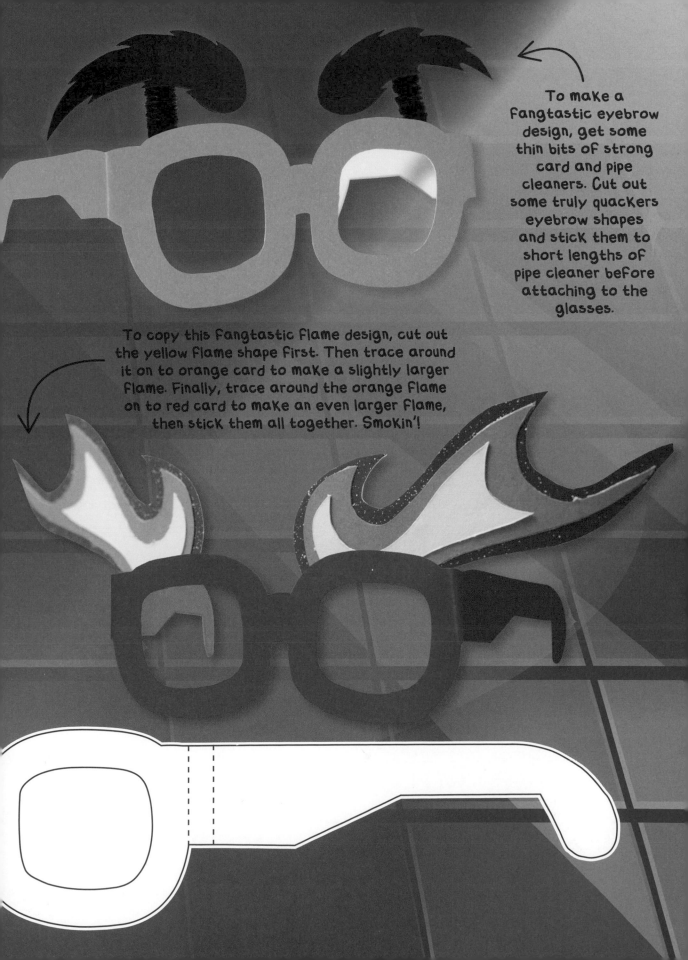

To make a fangtastic eyebrow design, get some thin bits of strong card and pipe cleaners. Cut out some truly quackers eyebrow shapes and stick them to short lengths of pipe cleaner before attaching to the glasses.

To copy this fangtastic flame design, cut out the yellow flame shape first. Then trace around it on to orange card to make a slightly larger flame. Finally, trace around the orange flame on to red card to make an even larger flame, then stick them all together. Smokin'!

78

Squidge Pumpkin Soup

This yummy supper is every bit as soup-er as a juicy neck to nibble!

You Will Need

1.25kg/2 ¼ lbs pumpkin or butternut squash, peeled, de-seeded and chopped into cubes
2 white onions, chopped
1 tbsp olive oil
2 tsp ground cumin
700ml/1 ¼ pints of vegetable stock
150ml/5fl oz double cream
Salt and pepper to taste
2 slices of white bread

Serves 2-4

1. Prepare your pumpkin and put the cubes in a bowl. Leave to one side.

2. Chop the onions and fry in a pan with the olive oil until soft but not brown. Add your cumin and fry for another minute. Add your cubed pumpkin to the pan and cook on a low heat for ten to fifteen minutes until they start to soften.

3. Add your stock to the pan and simmer for fifteen minutes until the pumpkin is soft all the way through.

4. Remove the pan from the heat, leave to cool for five minutes before adding your cream and blending until smooth. Add salt and pepper to taste.

5. To make your shark-bread dippers, pop your slices of bread in the toaster until brown, carefully cut out your shark shapes, and serve with your soup.

MOSHI TIP

There is a lot of chopping in this recipe. Always ask an adult to help you when making this soup.

Snookums Marzipan Eggs

These eggs-ellent little treats will have everyone coming back for seconds. And thirds . . . and fourths . . .! Goo-pendous!

You Will Need

250g/9oz white marzipan
100g/3½oz white chocolate, melted
Hundreds and thousands
Edible glitter
Jelly sweets
Selection of food colouring

Makes approximately 12 eggs, depending on the size you want

1. Use your hands to shape your pieces of marzipan into eggs. We made them half the size of a normal egg.

2. Dip your eggs into the melted chocolate, place them on a baking tray lined with baking paper, then sprinkle on your decorations. Let them set, then eat! Fangtastic!

MOSHI TIP

Try using milk, dark or white chocolate to dip your eggs. Or why not add food colouring to white chocolate to create your favourite colour!

DIY I.G.G.Y. Pillow

Want a cute cuddlesome Snaffler for your bedroom? Look no futher. And there's no pesky sewing involved!

You Will Need

Purple Fleece Fabric
(at least 1m square)
Pins
Scissors
Hollowfibre stuffing
Pen
White, black, purple
and pink Felt
PVA glue

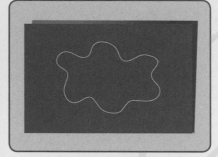

1. Fold the material in half. On one side of the fabric draw a spiky I.G.G.Y. shape. Make sure the spikes are curved instead of pointy.

2. Now draw a bigger version of the shape around the shape you've just drawn - about 7cm bigger.

3. Pin the two halves together. Cut out around the biggest shape.

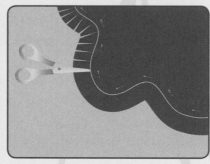

4. Now keeping the two layers together, create a fringe effect by making small cuts 2cm apart from the edge in to the inner shape you drew first.

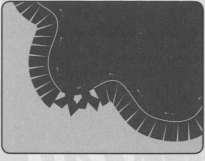

5. Double knot the fringe pieces together. Continue all the way around leaving a gap so you can push the stuffing in.

6. Push the hollowfibre stuffing into the cushion until it's nicely padded out. Tie the remaining fringes together.

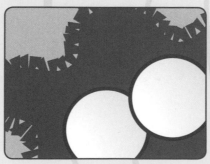

7. Cut out two large circles of purple felt and two slightly smaller circles of white felt to form I.G.G.Y.'s eyes and glue these in place.

8. Using the picture opposite as a guide, cut out crescent shapes of purple and black felt and stick them in place to complete the eyes. Glue on a small piece of pink felt to make I.G.G.Y.'s mouth

CocoLoco Juice Cup

You won't be able to stop sipping bongo-colada from your nutty Naughty Nutter head.

 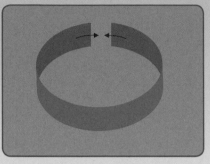 

You Will Need
Coconut
Saw
Card
Felt-tip pens
PVA glue

1. Ask an adult to saw off the top of the coconut. Pour away the milk and scoop out the insides.

2. Cut out a strip of card to make a circular stand for your coconut, by gluing both ends together.

3. Cut out card arms and glue to the base.

4. Draw eyes, mouth and cheeks on to card, cut them out and stick them to your coconut.

Fill with a delicous drink, add a straw and enjoy.

Egg Necklace

So you've adopted a Moshling, but where do you keep it? Well, here's how to take your favourite Moshling with you wherever you go . . .

1. Ask an adult to help you make holes in the top and bottom of two eggs. Blow through the hole to empty the egg. Cover both eggs in sticky tape.

2. Cover three quarters of each egg in papier maché and leave to dry.

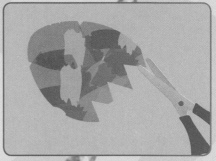

3. Carefully remove the eggs so only the papier maché shells remain. Cut a zig-zag edge round each egg.

4. Make a larger hole in the top of each papier maché egg and then paint inside and out.

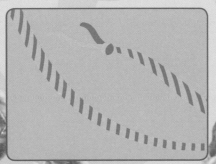

5. Make a long friendship chain using two strands of contrasting wool (see make number 54).

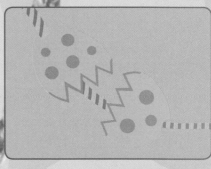

6. Thread both ends of the chain through the top of one egg and the bottom of the other and tie a knot at either end to keep the shells in place.

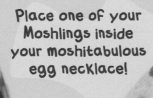

Place one of your Moshlings inside your moshitabulous egg necklace!

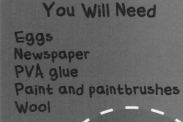

You Will Need

Eggs
Newspaper
PVA glue
Paint and paintbrushes
Wool

MOSHI TIP

Turn to make number 1 to see how to make papier maché!

Cap'n Buck's Pirate Stencil

Make this terrifyin' stencil. Arrgh! It'll send shivers up ye spine!

1. Trace the template of the skull and crossbones on to a piece of card.

2. Cut out the stencil skull shape and place on your paper.

3. Dab paint all over the holes in the stencil with a sponge. You're all shipshape now, me hearties!

You can use your stencil
pretty much anywhere – why
not try it on stationery or
napkins, or to make your own
pirate wrapping paper?

Missy Kix Dance

Here are just some of Missy's magical dance moves! Give them a go and then see what others you can come up with!

1. Put your hands in the air and shake your body left to right.

2. Clap your hands above your head to the beat.

3. Spin around, with your arms out.

4. Tap, tap, tap your feet. Keep it going to the beat.

5. Bring your arms back into the air to the beat.

6. Wave your arms in front of you.

7. Clap your hands above your head to the beat.

8. Point your thumb, shake your left arm. Repeat with other arm.

9. Wave your arms in front of you, back and forth.

Are you ready for the show?
Shake your body to and fro
Clap your hands and feel the flow
Then spin around
Don't get flustered by the beat
Let the music guide your feet
Reconfigure then delete
Let's hit the street

Every Moshi's talking about the latest thing
But I just wanna boogie, party and sing
Every Moshi's talking about the latest thing
And guess what's in?

Leader of the fashion pack
I'm pumping up the glam
But other acts just wanna throw their toys out of
the pram
Can you keep a secret I'm a Moshi on a mission
I'm Missy Kix, the sassy secret agent/musician

Every Moshi's talking about the latest thing
But I just wanna boogie, party and sing
Every Moshi's talking about the latest thing
And guess what's in? The Missy Kix Dance!

Chorus:
Aa-ah aah, you gotta jump on in
Aa-ah aah, the Missy Kix Dance!
Aa-ah aah, you gotta jump and spin
So jump right in, the Missy Kix dance!

I'm a chic but deadly beauty
I'm a star that's set to stun

You can call me when you need me,
I can be your number one
When danger comes a knocking you'll know
just who to ring
I'm Missy Kix the undercover Moshi
who can sing

Every Moshi's talking about the latest thing
But I just wanna boogie, party and sing
Every Moshi's talking bout the latest thing
And guess what's in? The Missy Kix Dance!

Chorus Repeat

Are you ready for the show?
Shake your body to and fro
Clap your hands and feel the flow
Then spin around
Don't get flustered by the beat

Let the music guide your feet
Reconfigure then delete
Let's hit the street

Every Moshi's talking about the latest thing
But I just wanna boogie, party and sing
Every Moshi's talking about the latest thing
And guess what's in? The Missy Kix Dance

Chorus Repeat

The Missy Kix
The Missy Kix
The Missy Kix Dance!

Gift Boxes

Here's how to make a monsterific gift box!

You Will Need

Selection of paper
PVA glue
Hole punch
Sticky tape
Ribbon
Scissors

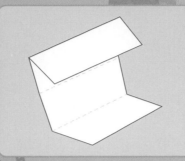

1. Fold a rectangular piece of paper in half, then fold each half in on itself so both ends meet in the middle.

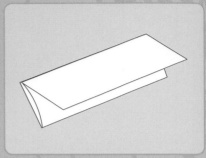

2. Open the paper out. Now fold the paper into thirds in the opposite direction of your first folds.

3. Open the paper out again. The creases should look like this.

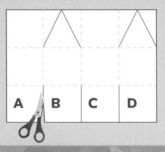

4. Cut along the crease lines highlighted and cut out the triangles as show in the picture above.

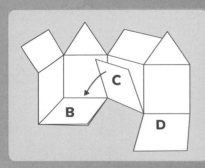

5. Fold and glue flap B onto flap A, flap C onto flap B and flap D onto flap C.

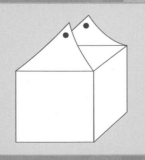

6. Finally, place your gift inside and then seal the open edge with sticky tape on the inside. Make a hole at the top of both triangles and tie with a ribbon.

MOSHI TIP

Why not use your moshitabulous gift paper from make 31 to make your gift boxes?

Gift Bags

Impress your furry friends with these clawsome gift bags.

You Will Need

Selection of paper
PVA glue
Hole punch
Ribbon or pipe
  cleaners

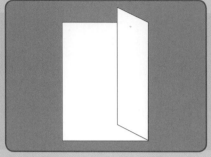

1. Fold a rectangular piece of paper in by about one quarter of its length. Run your thumbnail along the fold to mark it well.

2. Turn the folded sheet of paper over and apply glue to one end.

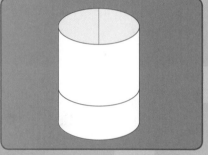

3. Glue the edges together to form a cylinder shape. Allow the glue to dry.

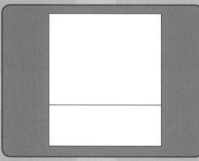

4. Flatten the cylinder shape, then run your thumbnail along the edges to make a good fold.

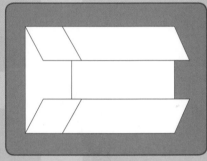

5. Fold about one quarter over on each side.

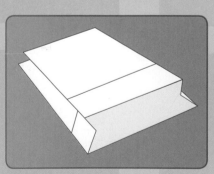

6. Open the two folds and press them inwards. You should now have a bag shape.

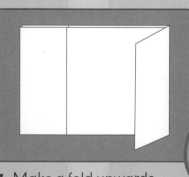

7. Make a fold upwards for the base of the bag. Glue it down.

8. Use a hole punch to make holes in both sides of the top open end of your bag. Thread ribbon or pipe cleaners through the holes to make the handles.

moshi monsters™

MOSHI TIP

Why not trace and colour the Moshi Monsters logo to stick on your gift bags or boxes?

Raarghly's Monsters and Ladder.

You can try, but you'll never beat that Moshi gaming geek, Raarghly, at this goopendous game!

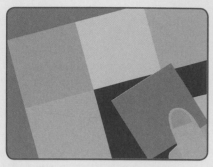

1. Measure and cut eight rectangles (6cm by 4.5cm) out of each of your foam sheets, to make thirty-two in total. Glue alternate colour rectangles on to the thick black card.

2. Put the numbered stickers on each rectangle, starting at the bottom left and zig-zagging to finish at the top left.

3. Cut ladders out of different coloured foam in varying lengths. Glue on to your game board so that each one joins two numbered spaces.

4. Cut different length snakes out of coloured foam. Stick on wobbly eyes and glue the snakes on to the game board, again so that each one joins two numbered spaces.

5. Glue 5mm wide strips of black card to the board to form grid lines.

How to play.

1. Take it in turns to roll the dice.

2. If you land on a space at the bottom of a ladder, move your counter up the ladder to the space at the top of it.

3. If you land on a space with a snake head on it, slide down the body to the space at the bottom of it.

4. The first person to reach number 32 is the winner. Fangtastic!

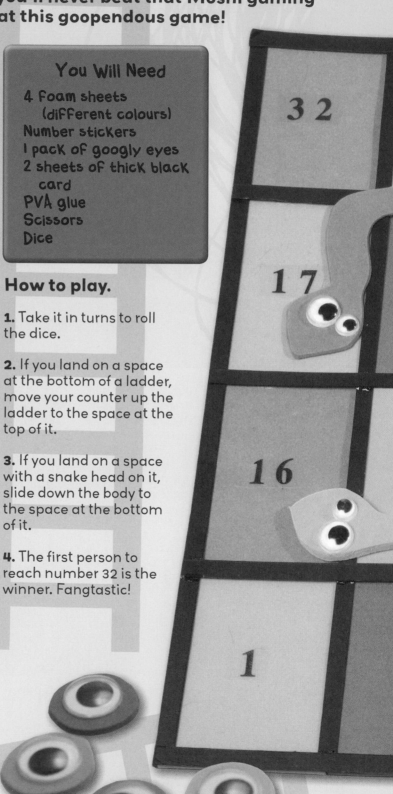

MOSHI TIP
Cut out four
different coloured
foam circles and stick
a googly eye on each
to make counters.

30 29 28 27

9 20 21 22

14 13 12 11

3 4 5 6

Pepper Popcorn and Slopcorn

Dig into the most funky, gunky movie snacks around!

For Slopcorn You Will Need

2 tbsp golden syrup
50g/1¾oz butter
50g/1¾oz brown sugar
½ tsp cinnamon
150g/5½oz pre-popped
or microwave
popped popcorn

Makes one bowl or box

1. Put the syrup, butter, brown sugar and cinnamon in a pan and melt over a low heat for two minutes, or until the sugar has completely dissolved. Keep stirring the mixture continuously. This will get very hot so you must make sure that an adult helps you at all times.

2. Once ready, switch off the heat and leave the mixture to cool for five minutes.

3. When the mixture has cooled, tip your popcorn into a large bowl, pour over the toffee mixture and stir well until the popcorn is evenly coated.

4. Pour your popcorn into a bowl or popcorn box, leave to cool, and enjoy! Yummy!

Log in to **MOSHIMONSTERS.COM**, click the **ENTER SECRET CODE** button and type the **name of the Moshling in make 75.** Your surprise free gift will appear in your treasure chest!

For Pepper Popcorn You Will Need

- 1 tbsp mild curry powder
- ¼ tsp salt
- ¼ tsp Freshly ground black pepper
- 1 tsp turmeric
- 25g/1oz butter
- 150g/5½oz pre-popped or microwave popped popcorn

Makes one bowl or box

1. Mix all of the seasonings together in a small bowl and leave to one side.

2. Melt the butter in a pan and switch off the heat, add your seasoning mixture and stir. Ask an adult to help you.

3. Tip your popcorn into a large bowl, pour over the spice mix and stir well until the popcorn is evenly coated.

4. Leave to cool for five minutes before serving. Sizzlin' hot!

Lady Meowford's Bag

Customize your own impossibly charming canvas bag. Purr-fect!

1. Trace over the image of Lady Meowford on this page and use as a template to cut her purr-fect shape from your fabric.

2. Cut two hearts from the same fabric.

3. Use fabric glue to stick your shapes into position.

4. Use contrasting coloured thread to blanket stitch around the fabric edges.

Glue on some gems to make your bag as pretty as a Kittie!

You Will Need

Ironed canvas tote bag
Patterned Fabric
Fabric glue
Embroidery thread
Gems
PVA glue
Scissors
Needle

Blanket Stitch

1. To do the blanket stitch, start by poking a needle and thread up through the inside of the bag just below the edge of your patterned material patch.

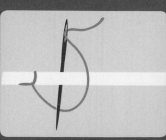

2. Poke your needle back down through both the patch and the bag, about 1/8 inch inside the edge of the patch and a tiny bit over to the right.

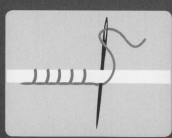

3. As you bring the needle back through the bag at the patch's edge (this should be just to the right of your first stitch), make sure to pull the needle through the loop of thread. Repeat as you work your way around the patch.

Dinky Dangling Fluffies

Don't hang about! Have lots of dreamy fun making these cute gangly danglers!

1. Using felt-tip pens, draw your Moshling's head and body on to card. Draw the hands and feet on a separate piece of card.

2. Colour everything in with coloured pencils and cut out carefully.

3. Cut two lengths of string for the legs and tape to the feet. Then tape these to the back of the card.

MOSHI TIP
The straw keeps your monster's body rigid, so don't skip this step!

4. Cut the straw to just slightly smaller than the character and stick to the back of the card as shown above.

5. Cut one length of string for the arms, thread it through the straw and tape at each end. Attach hands to each end of the arm string, then stick a loop of string to the back at the top so you can hang your Moshling up!

Use these pictures of Dipsy and Flumpy to help you draw the Fluffies on to your card.

You Will Need

White card
Felt-tip pens
Coloured pencils
String
Paint
Scissors
Sticky tape
A straw

Moshi House

Home sweet Moshi home! There's no place like home, so here's how to make your own monster crib!

You Will Need

Shoebox
Card
Mixed coloured paper
Brown parcel paper
Paints
PVA glue
Scissors
1 split pin
Ruler
Colour copy of the
  Fireplace and painting

1. Cover your shoebox with brown paper and cut two windows out of the lid, putting some blue card behind them. Cut a curve for the door, leaving and bending one side as a hinge so it opens and closes.

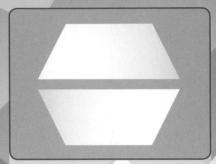

2. For the roof, cut out two identical pieces of strong card, as wide as your shoe box at the top, 5cm wider at the bottom and 15cm tall.

3. Cut out tiles and stick them down one by one on to both card roof pieces. Start at the bottom and work your way up.

4. Cut out a piece of card as long as the top of the roof, and about 2cm wide. Fold it in half and attatch to the top of the roof to join the two parts together.

5. Cut out two bits of card as wide as the top of the box, with a 2cm tab on each side. Fold up the tabs and stick them underneath the roof. Now it will balance on top!

6. Stick a small circle of coloured card to the door for a window. Push the split pin through it for a door handle.

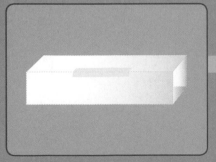

7. Measure the width of the door, then make a strip of card this wide and fold it round to make a step. Stick the step underneath the door.

8. To decorate the inside of you house, paint the wallpaper an flooring. Photocopy or trace the fireplace and painting templates on the next page to complete your room.

MOSHI TIP

Why not create a whole street of different houses for your Moshlings?

92 Warrior Wombat Glasses

Secret sleep goggles (so you can pretend to be awake when you're asleep!). Zzzzzz!

1. Photocopy or trace the eyes from this page and cut them out.

2. Put PVA glue on the back of the eyes and stick them in the middle of the lenses of the old glasses.

You Will Need

Access to a colour photocopier
Scissors
PVA glue
Paintbrush
Old glasses – 3D cinema glasses are perfect!

MOSHI TIP

Someone boring you? Wear these eye-tastic shades and always look alert!

Crazy Daisy Vase

Make this moshlingtastic cool vase and you never know, you may just catch some brand-new Moshlings!

You Will Need

1 jam jar
PVA glue
Coloured card
Different coloured felt
Buttons
Scissors

1. Wrap the coloured card around the jam jar, and glue the ends together to secure.

2. Cut out Craisy Daisy petal shapes from felt and stick to your vase in a flower pattern, alternating colours as you go.

3. Draw on a green stalk for each flower or cut them out from green card and stick them place.

4. Stick the buttons on to the centre of each Crazy Daisy flower.

MOSHI TIP

Half fill your jam jar with water, put your favourite flowers in it and wait . . . a little Moshling might be lurking near by!

Candy Cane Caves Cake

Whip up this splat-tastic sticky cake. Just make sure that sickly sweet villain doesn't get those sticky paws on it!

You Will Need

350g/12oz unsalted butter
350g/12oz caster sugar
8 eggs and 4 tsp vanilla extract (lightly beaten together)
360g/12¼oz self-raising flour
125g/4½oz cornflour, sifted
1 tsp each of red, yellow, green and blue food colourings
3 tbsp strawberry jam for the filling
4 cake tins

Butter icing
300g/10oz unsalted butter, room temperature
675g/1½oz icing sugar
3 tsp strawberry flavouring
1 tbsp milk
2 drops pink food colouring

To decorate
Your favourite sweets!

Serves 8-10 people

1. Preheat your oven to 190°C/Gas Mark 5. Grease and line four 20-cm/8-inch cake tins with baking paper.

2. Cream together the butter and sugar until light and fluffy, and gradually add your egg mixture a little at a time. Add 1 tbsp of your measured flour to the mixture if it starts to curdle.

3. Using a large metal spoon, fold in your flour and cornflour until fully mixed.

4. Split the mixture evenly between four small bowls and add your chosen colours to each one. Stir until the cake mixture is evenly coloured.

5. Spoon each batch of mixture into its own cake tin and spread it out evenly. Ask an adult to bake it in the oven for twenty to twenty-five minutes until springy to the touch and the cake is shrinking slightly from the side of the tin. Once ready, take the cakes out of the oven, remove from the tins, and leave to cool on a wire rack.

6. While the cakes cool, make your icing by beating together the butter and icing sugar until light and fluffy. Add your strawberry flavouring and colouring and mix until fully combined.

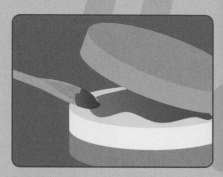

7. When completely cooled, you can start to layer your cakes. Evenly spread each layer with 1 tbsp of jam and a little of the icing. Repeat until you put your last cake on the top.

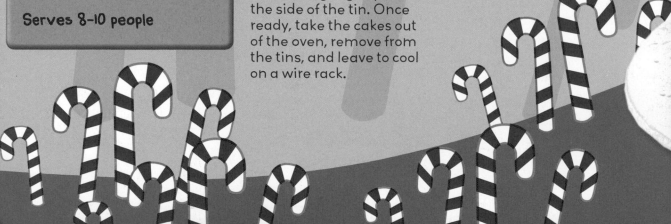

9. Now decorate your cake with all of your favourite sweets and make it look like the crazy Candy Cane Caves! Finish off with some edible glitter and a sprinkling of popping candy to give your cake a fangtastic fizz!

8. Carefully cover your cake with the strawberry icing using a pallet knife or a plastic spatula. You can make the icing look as messy and spiky as you want.

WARNING! Character cut-outs (see next page) should not be placed in direct contact with your cake.

MOSHI TIP

Here are some colourful characters to photocopy and cut out, to decorate your cake with. Glue the ones for the top on to cocktail sticks. Don't forget to remove them before you eat it though!

Penny Money Box

Ker-ching! Make this mini money box, just be careful you don't lose it down the side of the sofa!

1. Grab a circular cream cheese box. Wrap masking tape around the edge to seal the lid in place.

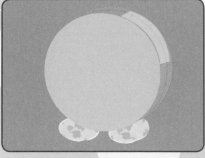

2. Scrunch up pieces of masking tape to form the rough shape of the feet and attach to the base, your penny box should now stand up.

You Will Need

Circular cream cheese portions box
Masking tape
Newspaper
Wallpaper paste
Paints
Paintbrush
Yellow card
Scissors

3. Tear up pieces of newspaper and using your wallpaper glue start adding layers of papier maché. Leave to dry for a day or two until it is solid.

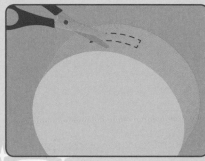

4. Cut a slot in the top of the box big enough to fit your pennies in. Paint the box as shown in the photo below.

5. Once the box is dry, cut out two arms and glue in place. Hey presto, you have your very own lucky Penny box!

MOSHI TIP

Find how to make papier mache in make number 1.

Honey Notebook
Just like Funny Bunnies, this journal is seriously stylish!

You Will Need

Notebook
Patterned paper or tissue paper
Multiple copies of the photo strip below
PVA glue
Scissors

1. Rip up or cut up your paper in pieces about 3cm x 3cm and cut up your photo strips to the sizes you want.

2. Use PVA glue to stick the paper clippings you have just torn and cut up all over the front cover of your notebook to make a colourful background.

3. Stick the pictures of Honey on to the background, keeping one full strip to one side.

4. Stick more pieces of coloured paper down, overlapping the pictures of Honey.

5. For the finishing touch, add the final full photo strip on top of your design as shown.

Fingerprint Purdy

Say meow to your own cute-ifal Tubby Huggishi! It's simply purr-fect.

You Will Need

Paints
Paper
Coloured pens
Paint brushes

1. For the body, press your thumb into pink paint and print it on a piece of white paper. Do a small fingerprint for the tail, then paint two ears.

2. When the paint is dry, add a bow with blue paint.

3. Paint a red spot for her tongue.

4. Then use lighter pink paint to add her paws and details to her face and and ears.

5. Now use a black pen to draw her eyes and nose. Then use coloured pens to add the outline detail. Mighty pur-dy!

This print was made with just a single finger print. Easy-peasy-gooberry-squeezy!

MOSHI TIP

Once you get the hang of it, why not create a whole Moshling collection?

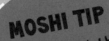

Ruby Scribblez Time Capsule

Make your past part of the future with this pawsome time capsule.

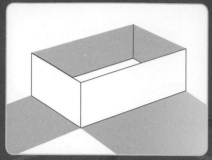

1. Wrap your shoebox with brown paper, and stick it down.

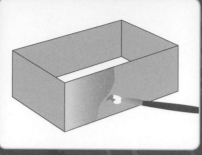

2. Paint the outside of your box grey or silver.

You Will Need

Shoebox
Brown paper
Grey or silver paint
Split pins
Photocopy of the label
   on this page
Craft knife

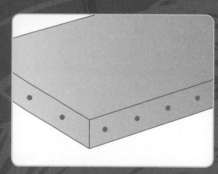

3. Get an adult to make little holes around the bottom of the side of the box, and around the sides of the lid.

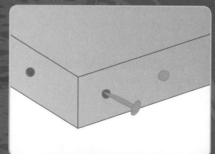

4. Now slot a split pin in each hole and open the pin to hold it in place.

5. Stick the label on top of the lid and write in your name, date of birth and the current date. Fill your box with personal treasures, then hide it somewhere safe to open up in the future!

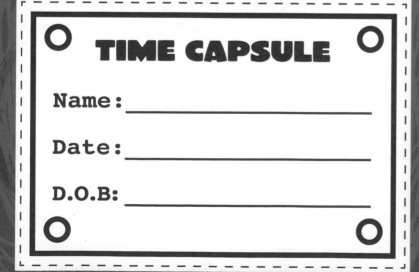

TIME CAPSULE

Name: _____

Date: _____

D.O.B: _____

Time capsule
label template

TIME CAPSULE

Name: Rebecca

Date: _____

D.O.B: _____

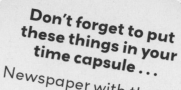

Don't forget to put these things in your time capsule . . .
- Newspaper with the date
- Photos
- Letter to your future self
- An old diary
- Lists of your fave things like music, movies, Moshis etc.

MOSHI TIP

If you don't want it to look like a metal filing box, you can pick whatever design you like.

Big Bad Bill

Snack Containers

Your friends will be monstrously jealous when you whip out your lunch in one of these!

1. Photocopy the templates on these two pages.

2. Colour in the blank templates and cut them out.

3. Cover the back of your template with a thin layer of PVA glue.

4. Stick your template down firmly onto your container and leave to dry.

You Will Need

A selection of plastic food containers
Scissors
Felt-tip pens
Coloured pencils
PVA glue
Sticky back plastic

This lunchbox belongs to

MOSHI·TIP
To make your
containers last longer,
cover the pictures with
sticky back plastic
so you can wipe
them clean.

This lunchbox belongs to

Mice Krispies

Eat these delicious treats before they snap, crackle and pop off!

1. Line a 22- x 33-cm/ 9 x13-inch baking tin with greaseproof paper and set to one side.

2. Put the butter into a saucepan and melt over a low heat. (Ask an adult to help you with this as the pan will get hot.) Once the butter has melted, add your marshmallows and stir continuously until they have completely melted.

3. Switch off the heat and pour your puffed rice cereal and hundreds and thousands into the pan and stir until combined.

MOSHI TIP

Try using black liquorice laces for the tails and whiskers too!

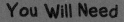

You Will Need

50g/1³/₄oz butter
200g/7oz pink
    marshmallows
150g/5¹/₂oz puffed
    rice cereal
Baking tin
Greaseproof paper

To decorate:
4 tbsp hundreds
    and thousands
1 pack pink liquorice laces
Raisins
1 small bag of jelly beans

Makes approximately
    12-24 mice, depending
    on the size you want

Eek! Did you hear something squeak?

4. Ask an adult to help you carefully pour the mixture into the prepared baking tin. Use the back of a wooden spoon to push the marshmallow mixture down into the tin until it is tightly packed in. Leave the mixture to cool down and set for 1½–2 hours.

5. Once the mixture is set, lift it out of the tin and peel away the greaseproof paper. Ask an adult to cut out the rectangles.

6. It's time to decorate your rectangles and turn them into mice! They should be sticky enough to keep the decorations in place. Sprinkle on the hundreds and thousands, then use your pink liquorice laces to make cute tails and long whiskers. Use the raisins for noses. You can then finish off your mice by adding two jelly bean ears to each one.

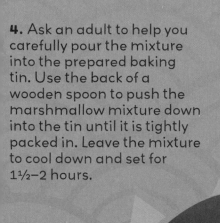

101 Ice-Scream Collage

I scream, you scream, we all scream for Ice-Scream!

You Will Need

- Corrugated card
- Patterned paper
- Coloured paper
- Card (for collage background)
- Acrylic paint
- Glitter
- PVA glue
- Scissors

MOSHI TIP

Use your Ice-Scream makes to create collages that look good enough to eat. Gloopendous!

Use lots of printed and painted paper to create yummy-looking ice creams.

Make the cones from corrugated card.

The top of this ice cream is painted with lots of acrylic paint and sprinkled with glitter.

MOSHI TIP

Draw and cut out a glass from paper to make an ice cream sundae